Help For Troubled Destinies

Taiwo Olusegun Ayeni

authorHOUSE®

AuthorHouse™
1663 Liberty Drive
Bloomington, IN 47403
www.authorhouse.com
Phone: 1-800-839-8640

First published by AuthorHouse   12/23/2009

ISBN: 978-1-4490-5857-9 (e)
ISBN: 978-1-4490-5855-5 (sc)
ISBN: 978-1-4490-5856-2 (hc)

Library of Congress Control Number: 2009913612
Printed in the United States of America
Bloomington, Indiana

This book is printed on acid-free paper.

Rehoboth Bible Ministries Inc Publications
2304 Oak Lane, 3A Suite 7,
Grand Prairie, Texas, 75051, USA
Tel: 1-. (972) 602-1837
Tel: 1- (972) 742-7365
Fax: 1-972-602-1837
Or
The Household of Faith Parish
The Redeemed Christian Church of God
5001 New York Avenue,
Arlington Texas, 76018, USA
Tel.:1-817-461-8857
Fax: 1- 817-676-9067
E-mail: taayeni@rehobothbministries.org
Website: www.rehobothbministries.org

Dedication

I dedicate this book to the Almighty God who stirred my heart in the direction of those crying out as a result of their seemingly helpless situation.

And to my late mother Mrs. Felicia Deleola Da-silva who in the process of confronting delayed destiny in prayer met with the Lord. Like Hannah when her Samuel eventually came after many years of waiting she had five other children thereafter to the glory of the Lord.

Acknowledgements

I wish to acknowledge the sacrificial support of my jewel of inestimable value Dr. (Mrs) Abidemi Olubisi Ayeni, my wife, who has continued to offer herself in order to see me succeed in ministry. Thank You.

To Rereloluwa Olusegun Ayeni (son) and Oreoluwa Olubisi Ayeni (daughter) who have both taken up adult responsibilities in the home in order for me to do what God has committed into my hand. You are blessed.

To Pastor Abiodun Coker, the Zonal Coordinator of Texas Zone 3, my pastor, friend and prayer partner who the Lord used to rigorously edit this work. God bless you richly sir.

And to all the churches of God, their pastors and brethren where I had preached these messages in various forms you are all appreciated. Keep fighting you shall see the tops of the mountains in Jesus name. Remain blessed and highly favored.

Contents

Dedication   v

Acknowledgements   vii

Preface   xi

PART I *In the Beginning......*   1

Chapter One Empowered to Succeed   3

Chapter Two God's Rescue Plan   13

PART II *"For though we walk in the flesh,*   17

Chapter Three Spiritual Warfare   19

PART III *I am Created to Fulfill Purpose.....*   39

Chapter Four Troubled Destinies I   41

Chapter Five Troubled Destinies II   59

Chapter Six Troubled Destinies III   71

Part IV *Upon Mount Zion........*   85

Chapter Seven Solution to Troubled Destinies   87

Chapter Eight Beautiful for Situation   97

Preface

Help for troubled destinies is a book I was inspired to write after having read and heard several messages generally written on destiny related issues without coming across one that specifically deals with the subject in modules that people can relate with. I believe dealing with this subject in general term is a disservice to the victims who are deeply overwhelmed by the happenings around them, also do not have specific details of the issues affecting their lives and therefore do not know what to do. This book is set to focus on these specific details by breaking them into identifiable modules with biblical and real life examples and solutions that people can relate with.

The book begins with the examination of what God did in the beginning, the foundation of empowerment He laid for us to excel, where we missed it and His follow-up plan. This in-depth background approach clearly shows us that we were empowered to succeed from the beginning as revealed in the divine encounter in Genesis Chapter 1:28. God blessed them and gave them five faith commands that they must follow in order to excel. These are: i) Be fruitful, and ii) multiply, and iii) replenish the earth, and iv) subdue it, and v) have dominion.

From this background and the understanding of the divine requirement for success, we should be able to comprehend why God had to introduce a rescue plan when man failed God as recorded in Psalm 82:5: ***"They know not, neither will they understand; they walk on in darkness: all the foundations of the earth are out of course."*** This should encourage us to respond to God's rescue plan of restoration to the paths of life by making the diligent efforts to Ascend, Stand, Abide and Dwell in His presence (Ps 24:3 and 15:1). By following these prayer steps the reader can regain, explore, enjoy and fulfill the five divine principles.

More importantly the book further introduces us to four core principles that can help a person to identify and fulfill his goals. These are the need to ***pray it, weigh it, say it*** and ***pay it.*** It introduces the importance of warfare, -even though we walk in the flesh, we war not after the flesh. Spiritually, warfare is crucial in stopping the onslaught of destiny terminators.

The next segment specifically identifies the various troubled destinies from the Bible with living examples that the readers can relate with. It ends with hope – God is beautiful for all situations (Ps. 48:1-2). It traces the biblical and real life testimonies of those whom the Lord broke through in their lives. This chapter rests solely on the fact that there is hope and help for troubled destinies.

May I therefore invite you to sit down at the Master's feet, as we prayerfully explore this book - ***Help for troubled Destinies***. Remain Blessed.

Taiwo Ayeni
January, 2009

PART I
In the Beginning……
"God Made man in His own Image" –
Genesis 1:26-28

Chapter One
Empowered to Succeed

"The earth is the Lord's and the fullness thereof, the world and all they that dwelleth in it" Psalm 24:1

Introduction

The plan of God for every man from the beginning is to succeed in life. Hence He deposited in us the seed of success. For this seed to work for us, it is our responsibility to identify, discover, activate and nurture it to fruition. Furthermore, we can assuredly say without any doubt that by pronouncing His blessing upon us in Genesis 1:28 He empowered us from the beginning to excel or succeed. However, it seems some people do not take cognizance of this divine package, and therefore have left it inactivated. Even some of those who recognize it do not know how to activate it. Yet, it is in recognizing its existence and knowing what to do with it that empowers the man who activates and cultivates the seed of success.

Whatever blessing that is available to a person but yet unknown and uncultivated, is like a man having a million dollar inheritance to his name and yet has no access to it. That life changing asset lays dormant, inaccessible and useless to its owner except it is utilized. Until it is activated, cultivated and applied, it cannot be said to have been enjoyed by him.

The place of discovery, of any spiritual blessing prepared for us by God, is in the presence of the Holy Spirit where we are ushered into divine mysteries. Many divine truths are left untapped because we are yet to pay the price to connect with them. The revelation and activation of truth inspires freedom to live well in his sight. When darkness stares at us in the place of light, something serious is happening in our lives and we must do something about it. We must fight to reposition ourselves to where we ought to be in Him. God does not give His pearls unto those who will waste it. He is willing to settle those who are willing to pay the price for change (Job 14:14).

The Earth is Given to Man

The Psalm of David Chapter 24:1 reads *"The earth is the Lord's and the fullness thereof, the world and all they that dwelleth in it"* The Psalmist through the Holy Spirit is calling our attention to important information. Not only does the earth belong to the Lord, the world and all they that dwell in it – we are also the Lord's as well. If this is so, whatever He, God owns as God, equally belongs to us through the covenant of Jesus' death and resurrection.

In fact, beyond the above Psalm several other scriptures proclaim our ownership and retainer-ship of the earth. Recall that God put Adam in the garden to *"...dress it and to keep it"* (Gen. 2:15). He was to harvest every fruit it yielded for him to enjoy. As long as he remained in fellowship with God, he was to enjoy all divine privileges promised to him by God but Adam after a while lost it through the temptation in the garden. Through this satanic scheme Satan took dominion from Adam, but Jesus through His death and resurrection claimed it back.

It was through this means that Jesus also took back the earth from Satan and gave its management back into our hands. This is confirmed in Psalm 115:16: *"The heaven, even the heavens, are the LORD's: but the earth hath he given to the children of men."* Whatever we make of our oversight of the earth is the outcome of what we see happening around us. When we fail to take dominion, terror or evil reigns and the foundations of the earth are out of course (Psalm 82:5).

We are supposed to take charge (82:2-4) and to appropriate the blessings and the fruit of increase it yields but because we lack the understanding of what belongs to us we are unable to lay claim to them. The Psalmist expresses strong thoughts in prayer requesting that God should take over because we have messed up our position just like Adam did. However, God is faithful to His words and He never fails. He has better plans than that and was unwilling to take that route. He has a rescue plan!

In a summary,

- The earth belongs to God.

  - Satan stole it but Jesus recovered it.

  - He gave it to us to possess. (Ps 115:16).

- It is for our inheritance (Ps. 25:12-13; 37:3,9-11, Mt 5:5)

- He created us to be in charge, to excel and be in dominion – Gen 1:27-28; Is 45:12 and Ps 110:2-3

- However we fell short of these five faith commands and as a result chaos set in – Ps 82:5/ Ps 11:1-2

God's Divine Mandate.

Before we begin to take a look at God's rescue plan for us what happened in the beginning? Recall the reasons God created man, and also see the confirmation in Isaiah 45:12 -13

"I have made the earth, and created man upon it: I, even my hands, have stretched out the heavens, and all their host have I commanded. I have raised him up in righteousness, and I will direct all his ways: he shall build my city, and he shall let go my captives, not for price nor reward, saith the LORD of hosts."

We were created to be in charge of God's creation and manage them. This was one reason God in Genesis 1:26 began a thought process of creating man in His image to have dominion over the heavens, sea and land. Notice it was a thought in God's mind that was verbalized. We can safely declare that this was God's *"Statement of Intent."* This defines what God had in mind to do.

It became a reality when on the sixth day He backed it with action by creating man (Gen 1:27). The eventual fulfillment of his intent could be said to be *"The Execution of His Intent"* We learnt this pattern of creative process from God. This is because every thought in a man's mind becomes a reality when it is backed with action. As long as it remains a thought without action very soon it will die. In verse 27 God acted on His thoughts *"…and God made man."*

Furthermore, in verse 28 He blessed man:

"And God blessed them, and God said unto them, Be fruitful, and multiply, and replenish the earth, and subdue it: and have dominion over the fish of the sea, and over the fowl of the air, and over every living thing that moveth upon the earth."

This is *"The Empowerment of the Produce of His Intent"* God equipped man to fulfill purpose and therefore he has no excuse.

The summary of God's commands is as follows:

1. Be fruitful
2. Multiply
3. Replenish
4. Subdue it
5. Have Dominion

The Five Faith Commands

1. Be fruitful.

God's divine expectation for man is to be fruitful. In fact, this desire is expressed all through the scriptures but declared in stronger terms in Leviticus 26:9: *"For I will have respect unto you, and make you fruitful, and multiply you, and establish my covenant with you."*

We can deduce from the above scripture that i) We are created to excel ii) We are empowered to excel and iii) We are covenanted to excel. God cannot compromise his desire for us to be fruitful. This explains why He puts the necessary things in place to guarantee our success. When the contrary is the case we see his wrath. That is why He cuts down any tree that does not bear fruit. We see a good example of fruitfulness established in the activities of the Lord when during the beginning of his ministry, he increased from 1 to 13 when you add him with the twelve and he never stopped there.

Just like the Lord was fruitful He expects us to increase or be fruitful. Increase however, must have its balance in the word. For example, there is an imbalance fruitfulness witnessed in Acts 6:7. While the word of God increased the people multiplied, yet the desire of God is as the people multiplied, the word also should multiply (Acts 12:24).

The after effect of this imbalance always reveals itself in gossiping, backbiting, murmuring and all sorts of character issues. This is because God's word from the pulpit has not been deeply formed in them. It has also not multiplied or bore the fruits of multiplication. The multiplied words of life in a believer give birth to unshakeable faith. The character issues manifested as a result of the imbalance are the fruits produced when the word is not multiplied in faith. *"And in those days, when the number of the disciples was multiplied, there arose a murmuring of the Grecians against the Hebrews......"* (Acts 6:1)

God desires the multiplication of the word in order to have a sustaining life within as the people multiply. This is to achieve a balance. The word must quicken, empower and separate the spirit from the flesh. The sword of the word must cut off excess flesh or else any imbalance of any sort would cause the flesh to show up. It is the continuous personal and pulpit exposure to the word of God that in the process of time makes the word become unto you *"wisdom, and righteousness, and sanctification, and redemption"* So that he that will glory would do so in the Lord and not in the flesh (I Cor. 1:30-31).

This situation always reveals itself or is especially prevalent where groups or crowd multiply over time and all we see there is the exaltation of showmanship and little or no serious place for the word of life. Here emphasis is given to entertainment, big choir, big drama, aesthetics and big building yet shallow minds.

The Apostles got it right when they chose to refocus the direction of affairs of the church by choosing seven Holy Ghost filled men to "serve tables" while they gave themselves *"..continually to prayer, and to the ministry of the word."* (Acts 6:4). Apostle Paul in defining the importance of the word in the same Acts of the Apostles Chapter 20:32 declared *"And now, brethren, I commend you to God, and to the*

word of his grace, which is able to build you up, and to give you an inheritance among all them which are sanctified."

2. Multiply

While fruitfulness or increase on its own is good, the desire of God according to his faith command is for you to move to the next level – multiply. There is great gain in multiplication and the advantage is that it guarantees a great leap in number and size of what we possess. For example, the disciples grew from 12, to 70, 120, 500, 5000, 7000 and a great multitude. When a man multiplies he grows in leaps and bounds. While increase is good it is no match to multiplication. One can increase in two ways- addition and multiplication. For example let us do a little addition and multiplication exercise:

Addition	Multiplication
2 + 2 = 4	2 x 2 = 4.

When you look at the table at this point they are at the same level. It will seem to the inexperienced that both addition and multiplication are the same. However, let us move on:

Addition	Multiplication
4 + 2 = 6	4 x 2 = 8

Now at this stage there is a slight difference. But as we move on it will become clearer. Now to the next stage:

Addition	Multiplication
6 + 2 = 8	8 x 2 = 16
8 + 2 = 10	16 x 2 = 32
10 + 2 =12	32 x 2 = 64.

At the end of the exercise the man with addition has a total of 12 while the man with multiplication has 64, a difference of 52. Can you now comprehend the clear advantage of multiplication? The reason why God desires multiplication should be very clear now having gone through this exercise. May the Lord multiply you in Jesus name.

The need to multiply with God is non-negotiable. It is in His nature to multiply that which you place in His hands because He is a God of multiplication. He multiplied the two fishes and five loaves of bread – the multitude ate to their satisfaction and still had leftovers.

3. Replenish

This is to restore what was used up or stolen. The earth abhors a vacuum so what was lost or used up must be replaced. It is God's mandate for us to achieve. The system abhors a vacuum therefore there must be replenishment of that which has been used up. When wine ran out at the marriage in Cana, of Galilee there was a desperate need for replenishment but it was too late to get fresh supply of wine. This threw the hosts into panic but the mother of Jesus was there to assist them in the rescue out of shame that this lack might cause. She said to the Lord "*They have no wine.*" (Jn. 2:3).

The Lord resisted the pressure to provide them with wine but it was a settled matter in the heart of Mary the intercessor as she was persuaded that He would do something about it when she asked. Therefore, without any further ado or plea she turned to the servants and said "*....Whatsoever he saith unto you, do it.*" (Jn. 2:5). That settled the matter and wine was provided by Jesus telling the servants to fill six pots with water and draw to give the governor of the feast. The interesting thing was that this new wine was better than the first and hence the ruler of the feast declared, not knowing it was water that was turned to wine, that "*....Every man at the beginning doth set forth good wine; and when men have well drunk, then that which is worse: but thou hast kept the good wine until now.*" Do you lack wine? Then go to Jesus and whatever He tells you do it.

4. Subdue the earth

Whatever gains we make through increase and multiplication can be lost if the earth is not subdued. That is why it is important to bring the earth under subjection so that one is not limited by it. The desires of nations have not come to pass because the earth remains unshaken. The book of Haggai 2:6-7 states:

"For thus saith the LORD of hosts; Yet once, it is a little while, and I will shake the heavens, and the earth, and the sea, and the dry land; And I will shake all nations, and the desire of all nations shall come.......:."

It is after these shakings that your desire will come and when it comes God will *"... fill this house with glory..."* This is because *"The silver is mine, and the gold is mine, saith the LORD of hosts."* (v8)

It is important to know that it is in fighting that you can possess. God gave Israel the lands of the Amorites and He told them in Deuteronomy 2:24:

"Rise ye up, take your journey, and pass over the river Arnon: behold, I have given into thine hand Sihon the Amorite, king of Heshbon, and his land: begin to possess it, and contend with him in battle."

The same principle is seen in the book Joshua 21:43:

"And the LORD gave unto Israel all the land which he sware to give unto their fathers; and they possessed it, and dwelt therein."

You cannot take possession or ownership except you fight. You can equally not subdue the earth and enjoy its blessings except you fight.

5. Have Dominion

When you are in dominion you are at advantage as the things of life submit to you. But it is not a place you can afford to take your eyes away from Jesus as this is the most vulnerable time in a man's life. Therefore you just must watch and pray so that the evil winds of life do not take you by surprise. The enemy you conquered is waiting on the sideline to regain what he lost in battle. He is watching with keen interest to pick on your error to strike at your weakness. His desire is to eat you raw and ensure you never attain to your destiny in life.

A good example is the story of Benhadad versus the king of Israel after suffering several defeats in the hand of Israel. His advisers told him we have heard that the kings of Israel are merciful kings, therefore send men to go and appease him maybe he might show you mercy. So he heeded their counsel and sent some of his servants.

"So they girded sackcloth on their loins, and put ropes on their heads, and came to the king of Israel, and said, Thy servant Benhadad saith, I pray thee, let me live. And he said, Is he yet alive? he is my brother. <u>Now the men did diligently observe whether any thing would come from him, and did hastily catch it: and they said, Thy brother Benhadad.</u> Then he said, Go ye, bring him. Then Benhadad came forth to him; and he caused him to come up into the chariot. And Ben-hadad said unto him, The cities, which my father took from thy father, I will restore; and thou shalt make streets for thee in Damascus, as my father made in Samaria. Then said Ahab, I will send thee away with this covenant. So he made a covenant with him, and sent him away." (I Kings 20:32-34)

The enemy is looking at your weakness to strike. Benhadad got a reprieve and because this aggressor was not tamed he struck again in 2 Kings 6:24 *"And it came to pass after this, that Benhadad king of Syria gathered all his host, and went up, and besieged Samaria."* The consequence was that women began to boil their own children to eat because of the famine that resulted (2 Kings 6:25-30). The King Ahab forgot he was the cause, and he therefore sent his men to go and punish Elisha the prophet because he felt he should have done something about it.

If Ahab had settled the matter of Benhadad once and for all at the time God put him in Israel's hands, the nation should not have gone through this terrible period in her history. Elisha did something as a result but it cost the life of the right hand man of the king who failed to believe (II Kings 7:1-2, 18-20). The toll of lives paid as a result of Ahab's carelessness was enormous. Prevention is better than cure so watch and pray as you enjoy dominion.

The Principles that Sustain Vision

Before we proceed further, what have you learnt from God's actions? We are aware that he gave action to his thought by saying it and paying the price to do it (Gen 1:26-28). This is broken down for us in four stages.

Whatever goal that is set for us before God can be said to be a vision and therefore for every vision to be realizable we must do the following:

- Pray it
- Weigh (Evaluate) it
- Say (Declare or Share) it
- Pay (the price) it

Recognizing and Fulfilling Vision

1. **Prayer** is one of the effective ways we communicate with God. It is also through this means we can discover what God has called us to do and the benefits He sets aside for us to enjoy. In a nutshell, prayer helps us to know His mind with respect to issues that affect our lives. Through this He orders our steps, guide and guard us through the path of life. *"**What man is he that feareth the LORD? him shall he teach in the way that he shall choose.**"* (Ps 25:12).

2. **Weighing or evaluating** the process helps one to identify the progress made so far and also have a clear understanding of whether the options chosen are working or going to work. Through this means one is able to identify how much resources are required to gain speed and which area is in dire need of that resource.

3. **Saying it** is sharing the vision with men of like passion in order for them to either support one either in kind or cash. As men are clear about the vision and where one is headed they throw their weight of support behind it.

4. **Paying it** is the willingness to keep going through the path the Lord is leading no matter how tough the way is – even when others do not get it. Nothing good comes easy – the price tag is always high. The way to the top is rough and hard but tough ones get there. Success comes with great sacrifices which include: self-denial, discipline, determination, dedication, and desperation.

Chapter Two
God's Rescue Plan

Who shall ascend into the hill of the LORD? or who shall stand in his holy place? (Ps. 24:3)

Lord, who shall abide in thy tabernacle? who shall dwell in thy holy hill? (Ps. 15:1)

Introduction

When God waited on man to fulfill the five mandates of Genesis 1:28 which specifically are: to be fruitful, multiply, replenish, subdue the earth and have dominion and when He saw that little or no progress was made He introduced a rescue plan. This rescue plan guarantees man's restoration to fellowship through sustainable prayer.

We see the following questions posed to man in the Psalms of David Chapter 24:3 and 15:1 quoted above. The summary is as follows:

- Who shall ascend?
- Who shall stand?
- Who shall abide?
- Who shall dwell?

1. *Who Shall Ascend?* (Col 3:1-4; Lam 5:18)

The need to ascend in prayer cannot be compromised and it is not by any means an easy task in itself. It requires grace to maintain an upward focus in the place of prayer. The challenge of Colossians 3:1 is *"If ye be risen with Christ, set your minds on the things that are above...."*

Many get shot down or cut off as they ascend in prayer through thoughts flowing through their minds, unexpected telephone calls or visitors and distractions of all sort from children etc. The antidote that the Master gives is to go into your closet and lock up to avoid distractions. Do not take telephone into your prayer room or wherever you pray and do not pray within the reach of kids who will always come to distract you as you concentrate in prayer. Be deliberate, determined and disciplined as you set out on every daily "prayer exploit with the intention to ascend and get to the throne room of grace (Heb 4:16).

2. *Who Shall Stand?* (Eph 6:11, 14b)

While the challenge of some is not the need to ascend, it is majorly the ability to stand in His presence. They are severally inundated by satanic confrontations based on certain flaws in their lives hence they spend good time having sparing partnership with the devil who succeeds in putting them on the defensive. It is from one accusation to the other that by the time they eventually find breathing space to pray they have already been rattled.

In Romans Chapter 12:1-2, the appeal of Apostle Paul to the Church is for us to present our bodies as living sacrifices which is our reasonable service. We are advised not to conform to this world but be transformed through the renewing of our minds. The only way we can withstand the challenges or accusation of the enemy is to adhere to this scripture by becoming living sacrifices without spots or wrinkles. We should learn to confess and forsake known or unknown sins so that the enemy should not resist us as we stand in prayer as we see in the case of Joshua the son of Jozedech the High Priest(Zech 3:1-5)

3. *Who Shall Abide?* (Jn. 14:16-18; Rev 3:20)

Abiding in His presence requires a deliberate focus that ensures consistent victory in prayer. This is maintaining a continuous presence no matter the pressure. All hell may break loose in respect of demands for our time or attention, our face or ears or whatever may be the case. The man who is determined to abide in His presence must be ready to shun all these pressures.

The disciples came to Jesus and told Him all men want to see you. What was His response? ***"Except a corn of wheat falls to the ground and dies it abides alone."*** Self must die to these things in order to be productive. It has to be a deliberate effort to win so that one is not tossed about by every wind of demand.

4. *Who Shall Dwell?* (Jn. 14:23)

This is having a permanent presence with him no matter the cost. This is the knitting of one's heart to His in the bond of fellowship. A prolonged dwelling in His presence is at a great cost but it is worth the try at the end of the day. The desire of God is for us to dwell, and we see the Psalmist in Chapter 23:6 expressing the desire to dwell in the house of the Lord forever.

The man who stays long in His presence enjoys the benefit of eating at the table of the Lord in the presence of his enemies. His head is anointed with oil till his cup of blessings over flow. To this one the assured goodness and mercy should follow him all the days of his life and he would dwell in the house of the Lord forever. The Psalmist emphasizes this because he was aware of the benefits it elicits or inspires.

Response to the Crucial Questions

The Psalmist responded adequately to the four crucial questions raised and they all predicated on character issues. The ones who could ascend, stand, abide and dwell are those with *"...clean hands, pure heart, who have not lifted up their soul to vanity, nor sworn deceitfully* (Ps 24:4). The others are those "..*who walk uprightly, work righteousness, speak the truth in his heart. He that does not backbite, nor does evil or takes a reproach against his neighbor. In whose eyes wicked people are condemned but he honors those who fear the Lord. He that swears to his own hurt and changes. He that does not put his money to usury nor take reward against the innocent."* (Ps 15:2-5).

These responses help us to have a clear understanding of the issues at stake. As long as one's character does not measure up with those who walk uprightly and work righteousness we will not be able to secure a glorious presence before His throne. He cannot behold the face of unrepentant sinners. The reason many are not dwelling is because they fail to connect with the four principles of divine restoration and fellowship. They want to have it their own way. The price of victory is high and one must be willing to pay it.

It is those who follow these principles that Psalmist tells us will receive the blessing (Ps 24:5). Which blessing? The blessing of Genesis 1:28 which is an empowering and enabling blessing to help one to be fruitful, multiply, replenish, subdue the earth and have dominion. Anyone that enjoys these five-fold blessings meets God's divine agenda for man. It is in God's plan to have us in dominion that we may eat the good of the land. These are the ones that would appropriate or effectively utilize the blessings as God holds their hands to subdue nations before them (Is 45:1-3; Ps 2:8).

Furthermore, they will enjoy righteousness or right standing in the presence of the Lord because of maintaining purity in His presence (Ps 24:4; 15:2-5). It is clear that blessed is the man whom God inputs no sin or his transgressions are forgiven. These men are fit instrument in God's hands ready to be used at any time. They do not require prop ups to fit in but are ready materials in His hands to do exploit in His name. Hence the reason God calls them Generation of Seekers in Psalm 24:6 (Mt 6:33; Is. 51:1-3) not Askers. The following highlights distinguish the difference between he who asks, seeks and knocks.

- Ask – Elementary level. Askers are babies. God expects something higher (John 4:23)

- Seek – Secondary (Kingdom mindset seeks not asks for the kingdom (Mt 6:33). Seeking requires diligence

- Knock – Tertiary. This is the level of spiritual warfare.

PART II

"For though we walk in the flesh,
we do not war after the flesh..........:
For the weapons of our warfare are not car-
nal, but mighty through God to the pulling
down of strong holds;" (II Cor. 10:3-5)

Chapter Three
Spiritual Warfare

"Lift up your heads, O ye gates; and be ye lift up, ye everlasting doors; and the King of glory shall come in. Who is this King of glory? The LORD strong and mighty, the LORD mighty in battle. Lift up your heads, O ye gates; even lift them up, ye everlasting doors; and the King of glory shall come in." (Ps 24:7-9)

Introduction

In the previous chapter, we learnt about how some men overcame the challenges of test of character and paid the price to dwell with God. These men were able to ascend, stand, abide and dwell in God's presence. The reward of God to them for their faithfulness in abiding with the word was to call them the generation of seekers (v6). Having paid the required price, God also proceeded to give them the encouraging incentives of being the ones that would receive the blessing and also enjoy right standing in His presence (Ps 24:5). They met all the conditions required to graduate into spiritual warfare.

Hence, it is no surprise that in verse 7 of Psalm 24 the Lord introduced them to spiritual warfare. *"Lift up your heads, O ye gates; and be ye lift up, ye everlasting doors; and the King of glory shall come in."* (Ps 24:7). This is quite instructive because God confronted the gates and everlasting doors that have posed ancient resistance to the breakthroughs of men. He was direct in His attack on these entities of darkness without mincing words. One thing to note here is the fact that He dealt with both gates and everlasting doors. Does this reveal to us there is something we have been missing out?

I have heard so much about gates but little or nothing about everlasting doors, yet it is equally as potent. There are many who have gained possession of the city gate yet the door of the city's blessings has been shut against them. No wonder in Zechariah 11:1 there was the aggressive war cry against the doors of Lebanon *"Open thy doors, O Lebanon, that the fire may devour thy cedars."* The man leading the aggressive prayer had the understanding that it was not just the gate of the city that needed to be uprooted but its doors as well if he must enter through the doors of favor, goodness, mercy wealth and greatness. Evil doors have succeeded in shutting out both children and strangers within communities out of their destinies because they are ignorant of what they are capable of doing. Therefore we must seek to learn and be spiritually aware or conscious of our environment.

Entities of Darkness

At this point, it is important to note that there are several agencies of darkness that every believer must be aware of and should also be willing to deal with in order to enjoy the blessing God has set aside for them. Many destinies have been affected and terminated as a result of our ignorance or nonchalance. These spirits operate with impunity and render many useless from attaining to divine promises. The specific job assignments of these forces are to kill, to steal and to destroy. The degree to which they attack a person, family, city or nation depends on the mandate received from the principal spirits set over them.

In conjunction with altars of affliction, we will briefly examine the following forces of darkness: Gates, Everlasting Doors, Idolatry, Thrones, and Handwriting of Ordinances. The understanding of their operations is important for the comprehension of the subject matter – *Help for Troubled Destinies.* This brief examination is a peep into their operations and manifestations in the lives of many believers. Ignorance is a strong weapon they wield in order to afflict the people of God. The knowledge we receive as we study them should equip us to build some level of war arsenal against them as we confront them in warfare. To engage them without being fully prepared will be suicidal.

Altars of Affliction

While evil altars are raised to afflict, righteous altars connect God's children with blessings. Altars are powerful instruments that connect worshippers with the spirit world. Because it is a place of trafficking of spirits one can contact spirits through raising formidable altars like Balaam did. The potency of the operations of forces of darkness is enhanced by the power behind altars. Without potent altars their powers are rendered null and void.

Evil altars are serviced and empowered by the priests behind them, and lend credence, sustenance and force to the powers of darkness. Without formidable altars the operations of evil forces will lack potency and hence be ineffective. Potent altars are gateways to the spirit world, a place where spirits traffic and make point of contact with God. Altars could be used to:

i) Indoctrinate/Control (e.g. Jezebel vs Ahab),

ii) Intimidate (Jezebel vs Elijah),

iii) Manipulate (Jezebel vs Elders)

iv) Dominate (Jezebel and Elders vs Nabaoth).

The summary of satanic altars is that they afflict. This was the reason Balaak invited Balaam to curse God's children in Numbers 22, 23 and 24. But God forestalled the madness of a prophet **"...who loved the wages of unrighteousness."** (II Pet. 2:15). There is the **way of Balaam** (II Peter 2:15), the **error of Balaam** (Jude 1:11), and the **doctrine of Balaam** (Rev 2:14). One needs to pray as an instrument in the Lord's hand not to walk in Balaam's ways. And as many who have begun on these paths there is time to repent, so that you do not end like Balaam.

As mentioned earlier, righteous altars are points of contacts for blessing, places of cutting covenants and also instrument of dealing with the forces of darkness. In I Samuel 7:7-10 Samuel raised a potent altar against the Philistines when the children of Israel after the national confession and repentance service led by Samuel said unto him not to stop praying for them and to cry to God to deliver them out of the hands of the Philistines (v2-6, 8). What happened before the cry was that **"....when the Philistines heard that the children of Israel were gathered together to Mizpeh, the lords of the Philistines went up against Israel. And when the children of Israel heard it, they were afraid of the Philistines."**

Furthermore, Samuel offered a suckling lamb unto God upon that altar: ***"And as Samuel was offering up the burnt offering, the Philistines drew near to battle against Israel: but the LORD thundered with a great thunder on that day upon the Philistines, and discomfited them; and they were smitten before Israel."*** (v10). From this account we saw that the effect of the altar raised against the Philistines brought devastating result. God thundered from heaven against them.

There was also the king of Edom who raised an altar of affliction against Israel by sacrificing his eldest son upon an altar and there was a great indignation as a result. ***"Then he took his eldest son that should have reigned in his stead, and offered him for a burnt offering upon the wall. And there was great indignation against Israel: and they departed from him, and returned to their own land."*** (II Kings 3:27).

The altar of Jaazaniah brought anger from God against 70 wicked elders of a city. These were altars raised in rebellion against God and to afflict God's people. ***"And there stood before them seventy men of the ancients of the house of Israel, and in the midst of them stood Jaazaniah the son of Shaphan, with every man his censer in his hand; and a thick cloud of incense went up. Then said he unto me, Son of man, hast thou seen what the ancients of the house of Israel do in the dark, every man in the chambers of his imagery? for they say, the LORD seeth us not; the LORD hath forsaken the earth."*** (Ezek 8:11-12).

In the same book of Ezekiel we read how men raised wicked image of jealousy against God with the intent of driving him from His own house. ***"Then said he unto me, Son of man, lift up thine eyes now the way toward the north. So I lifted up mine eyes the way toward the north, and behold northward at the gate of the altar this image of jealousy in the entry. He said furthermore unto me, Son of man, seest thou what they do? even the great abominations that the house of Israel committeth here, that I should go far off from my sanctuary? but turn thee yet again, and thou shalt see greater abominations."*** (Ezek 8:5-6)

In similar manner, evil people could raise altars against us and several elements could be used e.g. names, effigies, pictures, blood, feces, spit, hair, finger nails, clothes, money that belong to a person can be used to afflict. All they need to do is to take any of these things to satanic altars and put forward their request for affliction and it is done. If any of these elements are thrown in water (marine), forest, land, or tied to your star (astral) or thrown in the air, they are raised as marine, forest, terrestrial and astral altars.

Gates

Gates are spiritual entities or men who have unusual supernatural powers to hinder others from entering into their destiny or inheritance in life. The Bible gives us insight into the fact that men can actually shut out others from their inheritance because of the spiritual powers they have acquired over time. The importance of having dominion at the gate is clear in the Bible. That is the reason we see written there that we would possess the gates of our enemies. Possessing the gates of the enemy puts control in our hands and we are able to move on into our destiny. Our portions are secured even as the line falls upon us in pleasant places. I pray that your *"..seed shall possess the gate of his enemies;"* (Gen 22:17). *"And they blessed Rebekah, and said unto her, Thou art our sister, be thou the mother of thousands of millions, and let thy seed possess the gate of those which hate them."* (Gen 24:60).

Spiritual Gates exercise authority over its victims because of the supernatural power they possess. If it pleases it allows certain category of people to enter into their inheritances, while it hinders others from enjoying this privilege. The book of Ezekiel reveals to us the audacity of these entities of darkness and how 25 men of the elders rose up against the city. They devised mischief and gave wicked counsel in the city. *"Moreover the spirit lifted me up, and brought me unto the east gate of the LORD's house, which looketh eastward: and behold at the door of the gate five and twenty men; among whom I saw Jaazaniah the son of Azur, and Pelatiah the son of Benaiah, princes of the people. Then said he unto me, Son of man, these are the men that devise mischief, and give wicked counsel in this city: Which say, It is not near; let us build houses: this city is the caldron, and we be the flesh."* (Ezek 11:1-3)

Because they hold the territorial power of attorney to take decisions that are binding upon the people, most of the time they afflict and oppress them. They deny men the good things of life by erecting invisible barriers in their path to hinder them just like territorial spirits do. In a nutshell spiritual gates cause sorrow, tears and bloodshed to their hapless victims all over the world.

Spiritual Gates exercise controlling influence over people's social, political, educational and economic lives. Those who do not have existing covenant with God and do not know him as Lord and savior join cults, and occults in order to gain spiritual access into the city. Their profession only thrives because of their allegiance to the powers that be and when they default they go down in penury as fast as they rose up in wealth. In some communities, you just have to belong to thrive in certain professions because the city elders watch keenly at the gate of those cities.

We see an instance in Isaiah 14:31 where God fought against the leadership and the led because of their evil works. The Lord rendered divine retribution and rebuke: *"Howl o gate, cry o city"* (Is 14:31). The gate in reference above is the leadership and the city is the led. The Lord broke forth upon them in judgment and it was indeed a time of weeping and gnashing of teeth. *(For detailed information on Spiritual Gates, please refer to* Smashing the Gates of the enemy – **through strategic prayers**, *by the same author.)*

Everlasting Doors

The subject of everlasting doors is a mystery on its own. It is sufficient to understand that this is an area where the church has not paid much attention. There is so much concentration on gates at the expense of everlasting doors which is equally as potent. However, Zechariah by the Holy Spirit opened our eyes to the need to deal with everlasting doors: *"Open thy doors, O Lebanon, that the fire may devour thy cedars."* (Zech 11:1) Why did he have to do this? It is simply because he had received the understanding that there are many who have gained possession of the gates of the city wherein they live, yet the doors of favor, goodness and prosperity are still shut against them!

The Psalm of David treated both gates and doors in context, and one is not by any means left out. A man of understanding should know that it is not just the gate of the city that needs to be confronted but equally its doors as well. If one must gain access through the doors of favor, goodness, mercy wealth and greatness, there must be an aggressive resolve to enter the gates and the doors by force. Evil or ancient doors have succeeded in shutting out both children and strangers within communities out of their destinies because they are ignorant of the facts.

The story of Mephibosheth is a good case in point. Here was a prince shut out of destiny and left to rot away at Lodebar until David remembered his covenant with Jonathan. He was shut out of the place of destiny into obscurity. The son of a prince who himself was a prince yet access to royal privileges was shut against him and was about to die unknown and unsung. And worse still he was helpless and hopeless, desperately incapacitated and incarcerated by his physical challenge of being crippled. His state was a study in pity. He had lost so much self confidence to the point in which when he encountered David he referred to himself as *"....a dead dog."*

Furthermore, his will and courage were overwhelmed by the size of the household of his servant Ziba He was seriously outnumbered and intimidated in the house where his servant Ziba had 20 sons, 15 servants and with his unnumbered wives. This man stood no chance. Almost everything was against him but the mercy of God. Mercy made standing covenant to be remembered. The covenant of his father with David forced the door of kindness and favor to be opened unto him and he miraculously found himself back into the palace.

David himself was at the backside of the desert rearing his father's sheep. If not for the spirit of God several good things would have passed him by. When Samuel was sent to anoint one of Jesse's sons as the king the door of wickedness reared up its head but God spoke for him. In spite of his potentials of killing his lion and his bears he did not have the best he deserved. Even when he was anointed in the presence of his brethren, the city where he lived vomited him thereafter, as Saul chased him from pillar to post making a total of 32 attempts on his life. He was resigned into obscurity living in caves and tents, hiding in the trees and fields until God intervened for him. *"And David abode in the wilderness in strong holds, and remained in a mountain in the wilderness of Ziph. And Saul sought him every day, but God delivered him not into his hand."* (I Sam 23:14)

Eventually, it required three anointing for him to finally gain control of the throne. The first was the anointing in the midst of his brethren *"Then Samuel took the horn of oil, and anointed him in the midst of his brethren: and the Spirit of the LORD came upon David from that day forward. So Samuel rose up, and went to Ramah."* (I Sam 16:13)

The second was as a king over Judah, *"And the men of Judah came, and there they anointed David king over the house of Judah. And they told David, saying, That the men of Jabeshgilead were they that buried Saul."* (II Samuel 2:4).

The third was poured on him when he was made the king over all Israel *"So all the elders of Israel came to the king to Hebron; and king David made a league with them in Hebron before the LORD: and they anointed David king over Israel."* (II Sam 5:3)

A graphic example of the manifestation of everlasting doors is found in the gospel of Mark Chapter11 verses 1 to 7 where we read the account of a colt tied down by the door where two roads met. The colt was not supposed to be tied down. It was supposed to be in Jerusalem for the assignment of carrying Jesus into the city. Yet it was limited by being tied down in a village. The Lord sent them to go to the village where this animal was tied, and He instructed them to loose him and bring him.

"And when they came nigh to Jerusalem, unto Bethphage and Bethany, at the mount of Olives, he sendeth forth two of his disciples, And saith unto them, Go your way into the village over against you: and as soon as ye be entered into it, ye shall find a colt tied, whereon never man sat; loose him, and bring him. And if any man say unto you, Why do ye this? say ye that the Lord hath need of him; and

straightway he will send him hither. And they went their way, and found the colt tied by the door without in a place where two ways met; and they loose him. And certain of them that stood there said unto them, What do ye, loosing the colt? And they said unto them even as Jesus had commanded: and they let them go. And they brought the colt to Jesus, and cast their garments on him; and he sat upon him."

This colt had been hindered from fulfilling destiny until Jesus showed up. It was tied down unknown, unsung and uncelebrated, yet it had the potential of strength and no man had ever ridden on it. Notice that he was tied down in a village. There are many destinies tied down in many villages and yet the owners of such destinies are sweating it out in towns and cities of the world trying to make ends meet, living from pay check to pay check. In spite of the potentials and commitment to hard work, success has become an uphill task and they continue to wonder why.

Thank God the master showed up into the situation of the colt. Here it was by the door of destiny and it could not enter. The gate of the city did not resist him, he had easy admittance into the city, yet about the time he should enter into the blessing of the city the rope tying him allowed him as far as to the door. What can be more painful to hear that a man failed an exam by just one mark or point. Or you missed an opportunity for blessing by just a minute. Or your commercial flight just left a minute after your arrival at the airport and you are left stranded. Or the helper of your destiny just left after having waited for hours. What separated you from your breakthrough is just a minute – what a pity. Such is the experience of some.

The colt was eventually loosed and brought to the master. It carried the Lord in a triumphant entry into Jerusalem thus fulfilling destiny. It entered the capital city celebrated, partaking in the glory that was extended to the Lord. The unknown colt became known and recognized, and walking on clothes spread for the Lord. The door of the city opened of its own accord to admit it. God's divine intervention made this happen. That will be the story of the reader of this book in Jesus name.

Doors do not open of their own accord except someone confronts it. It is therefore no wonder that the Bible declares that *"Blessed is the man that heareth me, watching daily at my gates, waiting at the posts of my doors."* (Prov. 8:34) You just have to keep watching and praying. *"Enter his gates with thanksgiving and his courts with praise"* Ps 100:4

Idolatry

Idolatry is one deadly evil that touches almost everyone on the surface of the earth in one form or the other. Its subtlety in arresting the heart of men is outstanding. The end result of idolatry is that it confounds those who patronize it. (Ps 97:7). The dangerous consequences of engaging in idolatry are found all over the bible with lamentation of pain and sorrow trailing its victim (Ps 106:19; Ps 78:58-64).

This deadly evil affected the family of Abraham so badly that his father, Terah wasted away serving other gods on the other side of the flood (Josh 24:2). Furthermore, the family experienced four generations of barrenness as a result of idolatry - Sarah (Gen 11:30); Rebekah (Gen 25:21); Leah (Gen 29:31) and Rachel (Gen 30:22). Ecclesiastes 10:8 reveals to us the consequence of breaking the edge or divine covering *"He that breaketh the edge a serpent will bite"*. The serpent bit the family terribly for four generations.

Further reference to the destructive influence of idolatry is mentioned in Jeremiah 48:13 where the bible hints us that *"…the house of Israel was ashamed of Bethel their confidence"*. When was Bethel the confidence of Israel? This was when Jeroboam built two golden calves – one in Bethel and the other in Dan. He did this to discourage the people from going to Jerusalem to worship, because he was afraid he might lose them: *"And Jeroboam, said in his heart, Now shall the kingdom return to the house of David. If this people go up to do sacrifice in Jerusalem…."* (I Kings 12:26-27).

These calves he had raised not only became a lie to the people, but also a sin. The people went to worship before idols that they gave the glory of God to the creation of their own hands: *"…behold thy gods, O Israel, which brought thee up out of the land of Egypt"* (v28). This king dissuaded the people from worshipping God in the proper manner. The manner and mode of worship simply differed from God's ordained pattern. He made himself priests of the lowest of the people and made a mockery of priesthood. The timing ordained by God was not only altered, but he also ran the worship according to the imagination of his heart. He did whatever served his whims and caprices: ***"So he offered upon the altar which he had made in Bethel the fifteenth day of the eight month, even in the month which, even in the month which he had devised of his own heart: and ordained a feast unto the children of Israel: and he offered upon the altar, and burnt incense."*** (I Kings 12:23)

It is important to mention that idolatry is equated with the sin of rebellion, and God hates rebellion and pride. He resists the proud from afar off and just cannot stand them. As a result the same treatment of sending wandering spirit that caused Moab to wander was pronounced on Israel in Numbers 14 verse 33 because of idolatry: ***"And your children shall wander in the wilderness forty years, and bear your whoredoms, until your carcases be wasted in the wilderness."***

One significant thing observed in this scripture is the fact that the wandering spirit has an able deadly associate called **the generation waster**. In order to fulfill God's pronouncement upon them, the wandering spirit kept them going in circles for upward of thirty-eight years until they were all ***"..wasted in the wilderness" "And the space in which we came from Kadesh-barnea, until we were come over the brook Zered, was thirty and eight years; until all the generation of the men of war were wasted out from among the host, as the Lord sware unto them."*** (Deut. 2:14).

(Please refer to Dealing with Generation Wasters, by the same author for detailed information on this subject.)

Thrones

Thrones as we are aware are set for kings to sit upon to rule. However, every throne has foundation and powers backing it. A formidable throne is empowered by covenant and its power influences every one that sits on that throne. For example, every one that sat on the throne of David enjoyed the favor and promise of the Lord. Even when one of his sons Joram made the mistake of marrying one of the daughters of Ahab and was influenced to commit great evil in the Lord's sight, the Lord did not punish him because he remembered his covenant with David: *"And he walked in the way of the kings of Israel, as did the house of Ahab: for the daughter of Ahab was his wife: and he did evil in the sight of the LORD. Yet the LORD would not destroy Judah for David his servant's sake, as he promised him to give him alway a light, and to his children."* (II Kings 8:18-19)

However, the throne of Jeroboam is an epitome of evil, rebellion and pride against God. Hence, the throne procured evil for everyone that sat upon it. Of the 19 kings that sat on the throne 8 of them either committed suicide or were murdered. The throne witnessed a high turnover of civil unrest, coup and harvest of untimely deaths. The hallmark of that throne was exemplified in Ahaziah who was notoriously evil

"And he did evil in the sight of the LORD, and walked in the way of his father, and in the way of his mother, and in the way of Jeroboam the son of Nebat, who made Israel to sin:" (I Kings 22:52)

How does throne affect us? The fact is that: *"When the righteous are in authority, the people rejoice: but when the wicked beareth rule, the people mourn."* (Prov 29:2).

"As a roaring lion, and a ranging bear; so is a wicked ruler over the poor people." (Prov. 28:15).

We have seen this trend of wickedness all over the world. Is it in the former Soviet Empire, Apartheid South Africa, China, North Korea, Haiti, Uganda, Rwanda, Sudan, Liberia, Nigeria etc just to mention a few? These wicked rulers did so much damage in their various countries and made refugees of their citizens. The same account of wickedness is true in the Bible as we see in the following scriptures: *"For thus saith the Lord GOD, My people went down aforetime into Egypt to sojourn there; and the Assyrian oppressed them without cause."* (Is 52:4).

"And he gave them into the hand of the heathen; and they that hated them ruled over them." (Ps. 106:41).

"If the spirit of the ruler rise up against thee, leave not thy place; for yielding pacifieth great offences." Eccl 10:4

The dangerous effect of evil throne is that they withstand the work of God and plot evil against God's children. The Psalm of David Chapter 2 confirms this: *"The kings of the earth set themselves, and the rulers take counsel together, against the LORD, and against his anointed, saying, Let us break their bands asunder, and cast away their cords from us."* (v2-3). They have both the power of the throne and spiritual power to effect any evil they intend to carry out. We saw in the time of Jeroboam how he interjected the worship of God by setting up altars in Dan and Bethel. The same is true of Herod who in trying to alter destiny killed several innocent children and forced the parents of baby Jesus to flee and escape to Egypt.

According to the word of God a king is expected to rule in righteousness but contrary is the case all over the world. *"Behold, a king shall reign in righteousness, and princes shall rule in judgment."* (Is 32:1). Rulers sit upon the throne to bring either righteous or unrighteous judgment. *"For rulers are not a terror to good works, but to the evil. Wilt thou then not be afraid of the power? do that which is good, and thou shalt have praise of the same:"* (Rom 13:3)

Evil throne bears rule with fetish powers and bloodshed. For example, the throne of Pharaoh was backed by the powers of the dragon and frogs (Ezekiel 29:3) These are evil spirits that work miracles in the palace of kings (Rev 16:13). However, in due time, the judgment of God came upon the throne of Pharaoh and Pharaoh himself.

While evil kings are on rampage, God has set His own king upon His holy hill of Zion and all He is asking us to do is to: *"Ask of me, and I shall give thee the heathen for thine inheritance, and the uttermost parts of the earth for thy possession."* (Ps 2:8). He wants to restore power into our hands and this can only be done if we respond to the Lord with understanding. There are set directives He had given in dealing with the throne. God is a strategist and He had secured formidable weapons against their onslaught.

Hence, in Psalm 149 we read these words: *"Let the saints be joyful in glory: let them sing aloud upon their beds. Let the high praises of God be in their mouth, and a two-edged sword in their hand; To execute vengeance upon the heathen, and punishments upon the people; To bind their kings with chains, and their nobles with fetters of iron; To execute upon them the judgment written: this honour have all his saints. Praise ye the LORD."*

It is with the combination of high praises of God and the word, which is the sword of God, that we can overcome the throne. With these we can execute the judgment written: by wreaking vengeance on the heathen, punishment on the people, but bind the kings with chains and the nobles with fetters. Notice, for the people it is punishment but when it comes to the kings and nobles we require chains and fetters because they are terrible. Through our obedience *"The Lord at thy right hand shall strike through kings in the day of his wrath."* (Ps 110:5)

Hand Writing of Ordinances

The phrase handwriting of ordinances is found in the Epistle to the Colossians Chapter 2:14:*"Blotting out the handwriting of ordinances that was against us, which was contrary to us, and took it out of the way, nailing it to his cross; And having spoiled principalities and powers, he made a shew of them openly, triumphing over them in it."* What does this mean? These are hardcopy evidences of legislations or judgment received against us from our forefathers. They are parchment of evidences that the devil waves in request for judgment against us. These hardcopy evidences are contrary to us, and designed to cause us pain, hardship, loss or sorrow.

These handwritings were made on parchments, papers, wood, leather, back of trees, leaves, egg shells, water bodies, the sun, moon and stars etc just to mention a few. Some of these handwritings are invisible to ordinary eyes, while some are visible but may not make sense to the uninitiated reader. They are sealed and made good by covenant. They are written scripts that men walk according to their dictate. Ephesians

2:10 refers to this trend and it is the fact that we are *"....created in Christ Jesus unto good works, which God hath before ordained that we should walk in them."*

We are created to walk in divine ordinances, but when the contrary is the case evil ordinance is at work. It should be no surprise to you when you see men do what they do not want to do and they do so with fervor. This is because they are under the influences of ordinances, and they have found no place for resistance. This had worked and continues to work in the lives of many families and their generations.

In Jeremiah 17 verse 1 the Lord mentioned that *"The sin of Judah is written with a pen of iron, and with the point of a diamond: it is graven upon the table of their heart, and upon the horns of your altars;"* (Jer. 17:1). Why? So that it should be perpetually remembered until the Lord forgives them. Anything one does not want to forget is written down. That was one reason God wrote the Ten Commandments so that we could read it and not forget to do them.

Also because God did not want to forget the sin of Amalek God commanded Moses to write it down *"And the LORD said unto Moses, Write this for a memorial in a book, and rehearse it in the ears of Joshua: for I will utterly put out the remembrance of Amalek from under heaven."* (Ex 17:14). Did He carry out this intention? Yes He did in I Samuel 15:2-3 when He told Samuel He had remembered the sins of Amalek. He gave him specific instruction to tell King Saul to destroy Amalek from the face of the earth.

"Thus saith the LORD of hosts, I remember that which Amalek did to Israel, how he laid wait for him in the way, when he came up from Egypt. Now go and smite Amalek, and utterly destroy all that they have, and spare them not; but slay both man and woman, infant and suckling, ox and sheep, camel and ass." (I Sam 15:2-3)

Even though Saul went in partial obedience, he destroyed the bad things and left the choice ones intact including Agag the King of Amalek. For this reason, amongst others he began the process of the loss of the kingdom. Samuel later killed Agag and put an end to the hegemony of Amalek.

Another example of manifestation of the Handwriting of ordinances is the man Coniah who was written childless according to the instruction of the Lord.

"As I live, saith the LORD, though Coniah the son of Jehoiakim king of Judah were the signet upon my right hand, yet would I pluck thee thence;…Is this man Coniah a despised broken idol? is he a vessel wherein is no pleasure? wherefore are they cast out, he and his seed, and are cast into a land which they know not? O earth, earth, earth, hear the word of the LORD. Thus saith the LORD, Write ye this man childless, a man that shall not prosper in his days: for no man of his seed shall prosper, sitting upon the throne of David, and ruling any more in Judah." (Jer 31:24, 28-30).

That he should be written childless did not mean he would not have children all that it meant was that none of his children *"shall prosper,"* even if they sat *"upon the throne of David,"*

Significantly, he would produce vagabonds, truants, wayward and unserious children. Children he would never be proud of, and who he should love to hate and eventually disown because of their evil conduct. Those that could bring him sorrow till he found comfort in the embrace of death and rest peacefully in his grave.

Ii is important to know that in dealing with handwriting of ordinances, we should not only use the blood of Jesus but also recognize that *"…he is our peace, who hath made both one, and hath broken down the middle wall of partition between us; Having abolished in his flesh the enmity, even the law of commandments contained in ordinances; for to make in himself of twain one new man, so making peace; And that he might reconcile both unto God in one body by the cross, having slain the enmity thereby:"* (Eph 2:14-16)

Even though ordinances are established for us to walk in them, it is not like evil works, which have no place in the presence of God. According to Ephesians 2:10 referred to earlier, we have been created to do nothing else but good works but when we see evil works rearing its head in our conduct, and we have no power to resist it, - evil is at work against us. We need to cry out until we see our change come. This is because we have been ordained to walk in good works not evil. Hand writing of ordinances set men up to walk in evil conduct.

Ordinances of Time and Seasons

There are several other ordinances revealed in the Bible such as the ordinances of the day and night, winter and summer, cold and heat etc. God set them there for time and seasons. In Genesis 1:14-18 we see the ordinances of the sun, moon and stars. *And God said, Let there be lights in the firmament of the heaven to divide the day from the night; and let them be for signs, and for seasons, and for days, and years: And let them be for lights in the firmament of the heaven to give light upon the earth: and it was so. And God made two great lights; the greater light to rule the day, and the lesser light to rule the night: he made the stars also. And God set them in the firmament of the heaven to give light upon the earth, And to rule over the day and over the night, and to divide the light from the darkness: and God saw that it was good.*

The Lord also referred to these ordinances in Jeremiah 31:35-36:

"Thus saith the LORD, which giveth the sun for a light by day, and the ordinances of the moon and of the stars for a light by night, which divideth the sea when the waves thereof roar; The LORD of hosts is his name: If those ordinances depart from before me, saith the LORD, then the seed of Israel also shall cease from being a nation before me for ever."

It is noteworthy to note that none of the ordinances, whether that of the day nor night have ever failed. Not only are these elements set to dictate time and seasons they also speak into the lives of men. The Psalm of David Chapter 19:1-4 informs us that: *"The heavens declare the glory of God; and the firmament sheweth his handywork. Day unto day uttereth speech, and night unto night sheweth knowledge. There is no speech nor language, where their voice is not heard. Their line is gone out through all the earth, and their words to the end of the world. In them hath he set a tabernacle for the sun,"*

What are they speaking into your life – good or evil? It depends on which side of the divide you belong. To those who believe in following the dictates of Zodiac signs before they engage in meaningful ventures you are threading on dangerous grounds or fishing in troubled waters. Nothing good comes out of stargazing because it leads a man to walk on the road to destruction. Evil are been spoken to many lives who are gullible as we speak and they accept it without crying out for help.

However, we thank God for God's divine antidote to whatever the sun, moon or the stars may be speaking. The Psalm of David 121:5 reassures us that *"The LORD is thy keeper: the LORD is thy shade upon thy right hand. The sun shall not smite thee by day, nor the moon by night."*

Spoken Ordinances

While there are handwritten ordinances, there are also spoken ordinances. These are pronouncements made by powerful people against one's rise in life. Many have struggled under the influence of spoken ordinances. A key reference to this subject is Psalm 45:1-2 *"My heart is inditing a good matter: I speak of the things which I have made touching the king: my tongue is the pen of a ready writer …: grace is poured into thy lips: therefore God hath blessed thee for ever."*

Notice the words *grace is poured into thy lips.* This is where the power of judgment or influence comes from. One man speaks and a generation of innocent family members begins to labor over the words spoken. A good example is the case of Joshua versus the one who would rebuild Jericho. *"And Joshua adjured them at that time, saying, Cursed be the man before the LORD, that riseth up and buildeth this city Jericho: he shall lay the foundation thereof in his firstborn, and in his youngest son shall he set up the gates of it."* (Josh 6:26)

According to Bible account the man Hiel rose up to build the city and he paid dearly for it. He laid the foundation and his firstborn died and when he set up the gates his youngest son died according to the words of Joshua. *"In his days did Hiel the Bethelite build Jericho: he laid the foundation thereof in Abiram his firstborn, and set up the gates thereof in his youngest son Segub, according to the word of the LORD, which he spake by Joshua the son of Nun."* (I Kings 16:34).

We also see in Numbers 24:20, how Balaam the son of Beor spoke about Amalek for utter destruction. *"And when he looked on Amalek, he took up his parable, and said, Amalek was the first of the nations; but his latter end shall be that he perish for ever."* Amalek as it were received double dose of this affliction to confirm its designed destruction. Recall that as mentioned earlier God told Moses in Exodus 17:14 that Amalek would be completely destroyed and this was fulfilled in I Samuel Chapter 15 when God through Samuel sent Saul to go and destroy Amalek. We know the rest of the story.

We have seen and heard wicked men speak into the lives of innocent men and women with great consequences. The power of the tongue has been used to affect destinies adversely and many are yet to recover from the scourge of the tongue But my prayer for whosoever is going through this kind of oppression is that *"Thou shalt be hid from the scourge of the tongue:..."* (Job 5:21). May the Lord free you in Jesus name.

The influence of Territorial Spirits

The six entities of darkness reviewed are territorial in nature and they operate on a wide geographical sphere. Their job specification is to waste lives and properties of people in their geographical domain. The initial trap is the innocent allegiance of people to community gods, traditional festivals, rites and ceremonies. Some communities have certain traditional rites they offer to appease the gods of the land and some families are custodians and worshippers of these gods.

Some rites are mandatorily done at birth, naming, marriage, birthday, and town day ceremonies. Commonly practiced in the recent past were tribal marks or tattoos that make the people known by sight from people of other communities. These marks are known to differ from community to community and are specified by territorial powers as tokens of covenants between them and the people. Specifically, these marks are tokens of blood covenants with the territorial powers ruling over the community.

Through these activities they afflict generations of people with the same problems within a community and also down the family line. This becomes possible because everyone involved in such traditional activities is automatically under the curse of God and they suffer what is identified as generational or inherited curses and afflictions. Psalm 97 verse 7 says *"Confounded be all they that put their trust in idols.."*

There are communities where the people are noted for promiscuity, while others are largely untrustworthy. In the first, it is a known fad that a woman never dies married to one man. The usual scenario is that a woman may have four children with each having different fathers and is still in the business of having an alarming high turnover of lover boys. A particular life example reveals a home where a grandmother (who was a single mother) lived with her daughter (also a single mother) and has a granddaughter whose favorite pastime was offering herself as "a universal donor" to men. This grandchild, just barely out of the cradle, was well known to have broken every sense of restraints in the book and matched every adjective that her preys used to qualify her. Very soon she ended the same way those before her did, a single mother.

In case of those who are untrustworthy, when they tell you something you better put a rain check on it, or you may pay dearly for it because you can never find them to be reliable. The degree of affliction per family or person within the community may differ, but they are all generally the same. As per individual curses the way and manner in which great grandfather was afflicted, was the same way grandfather suffered and now in the fourth generation the great grandchild now a father is under the same affliction.

How do they mete out punishment to their victims? The spirits file away documents of satanic contracts or transactions and use them effectively, to deal legally with their victims when the need arises. These documents are reference points to the activities of the past, the promises made and responsibilities tied to it. Thus the covenant or contracts of the forefathers which have put several generations, born and unborn into perpetual bondage become legal evidences. Where there is default to these contracts or agreements the satanic entities move viciously against their recalcitrant but helpless victims in order to enforce compliance. In this they have continued to enjoy unhindered success except the victim engages them in spiritual warfare.

PART III

I am Created to Fulfill Purpose.....
"My Times are in thy hand: deliver me from the hand of mine enemies, and from them that persecute me." - (Ps 30:15)

Chapter Four
Troubled Destinies I

"Although affliction cometh not forth of the dust, neither doth trouble spring out of the ground; Yet man is born unto trouble, as the sparks fly upward. I would seek unto God, and unto God would I commit my cause" (Job 5:6-8)

Introduction

Job Chapter 5:6-8 introduces us to a peculiar situation that troubles the destiny of man. It opens our eyes to the fact that affliction does not drop down from the sky neither does it grow out of the ground, yet man is born into trouble. Chapter 14:1 of Job also corroborates this fact: ***"Everyone born of a woman is of a few days but full of trouble."*** Why this is so is beyond our comprehension.

Because of the grievous outcomes, the resolution of the man in Job 5 is if this is the lot of man then ***"I would seek unto God, and unto God would I commit my cause."*** (v8) This is a divinely inspired decision that reveals deep spiritual insight. The truth already affirmed here, is that the only way out of satanic affliction realistically is to seek God's help in prayer. It is through prayer that the oppressed can and will be delivered - ***"The righteous cry and the Lord heareth and delivereth them out of all their troubles."*** (Ps 34:17)

No matter the trouble we face when we know who to cry to our problems will receive divine attention or solution in spite of how numerous they may be. The Psalmist reassures us that: ***"Many are the afflictions of the righteous: but the LORD delivereth him out of them all."*** (Psalm 34:19) All God is looking for is a broken and contrite heart that is willing to submit to Him. The Lord is nigh unto such as possess these qualities. (v18)

Not only did he intend to seek God, he has also decided to commit his troubles unto Him. There is wisdom in this decision because as mentioned earlier it is the only way out of trouble. Many who lack understanding either try to explain away their problems or use carnal weapons to deal with them. Whichever option chosen will be met with failure, God is the only way out of trouble. Hence committing our cause unto Him is not an option – it is the only way out.

The Preacher in the book of Ecclesiastes made a profound observation that captures the present situation of some people, who have refused to face reality but continue to explain away their situations. As a result they prolong the cycle of oppression and give the oppressor the advantage. The Preacher calls it an evil under the sun. ***There is an evil which I have seen under the sun, as an error which proceedeth from the ruler: Folly is set in great dignity, and the rich sit in low place. I have seen servants upon horses, and princes walking as servants upon the earth.*** (Eccl.10:5-7)

Why is it an evil? It is because God has not called us to servitude but to dominion. In fact, the commands of God, amongst others are to subdue the earth and have dominion. It is therefore an evil thing to be found on the receiving end, in servitude, deprivation and domination. Not only that, but to now compound the matter by explaining it away is the worst excuse any child of God should make. The ruler is supposed to be in charge not to be ruled by tyranny. It is an error for princes to allow servants to take over, while foolishness is exalted in great dignity, and the rich sit in low places. This is an abomination. It is the case of the tail wagging the dog or the led leading the leader.

Servants have taken over the reign of leadership while the princes follow them on foot. It is a role reversal that has brought shame and defeat. It is a misplaced ideal that reeks of nothing but madness that has been given a voice against reasonable opinion. You see men in bondage trying to defend the indefensible while they say: **"You see it runs in the family, everybody is like that. As we approach fifty, we lose our wealth after rising to prominence. It is a family thing!"** They know it, they see it and expect it and nobody is willing to stop the "..*folly that is set in dignity...*"

The ruler ought to arise and say "Enough is enough" to this nonsense. Who is that ruler? You and I! As long as you have received Jesus as your Lord and savior – you are a king and priest raised through His death and resurrection. *And hath made us kings and priests unto God and his Father; to him be glory and dominion for ever and ever. Amen.* (Rev 1:6)

A ruler or a king does not beg to rule, he bears rule because he knows who he is and the power backing him. God has called us to dominion and we need to quickly respond or else the enemy will mar our destiny. We must maintain a sure ground of victory by seeking to know the truth as it pertains to why we are called. *"A man through knowledge shall deliver himself."*

Finding out the truth and confronting the enemy will stop the cycle of oppression and ensure you enjoy divine benefits. The good that will follow you is much more than what money can buy. It is for your own good if you do so. *"Lo this, we have searched it, so it is; hear it, and know thou it for thy good."* (Job 5:27). There is also wisdom in searching it out or observing it. The outcome is rewarding – *"Whoso is wise, and will observe these things, even they shall understand the lovingkindness of the LORD."* (Ps. 107:43)

Identifying Troubled Destines

There is a need to discover troubled destinies in good enough time and deal with it. Some people have left the issues of their lives hanging till it is too late before they cry out for help. Some foundations are faulty because of generational curse and except this is identified and broken the cycle continues. We see several examples in real life situations as well as in the Bible. For example, the destinies of Amalek were affected by two divine pronouncements as follows:

1. **From God:** *"And the LORD said unto Moses, Write this for a memorial in a book, and rehearse it in the ears of Joshua: for I will utterly put out the remembrance of Amalek from under heaven"* (Ex 17:14)

2. From Balaam, God' servant: *"Amalek was the first of the nations; but his latter end shall be that he perish for ever.* (Num 24:20).

A careful examination of these verses reveals that the destiny of Amalek had been settled no matter what they do or did not do. Both were prophetic declarations that had been set into motion by divine reckoning, and its execution was just a matter of time. In the process of time, however, God remembered His word concerning this doomed nation and he sent Saul via the instruction of Samuel to go and utterly destroy them (I Sam 15:2-3). But we know the rest of the story and how Saul disobeyed God and spared the choice things including Agag – the king of Amalek.

The foundation of a man affects his life. When God looks at a man, He looks beyond him and seeks to view his foundation. A man's rise and fall in life are tied to his foundation *"If the foundations be destroyed, what can the righteous do?"* (Ps 11:3). The foundation of spirituality, marriage, finances, business, relationship etc deeply matters. This determines how far it will go and the experience it will encounter. For example, the problem of King Jehoram the son of Jehoshaphat was tied to the foundation of his marriage. Not only was it recorded that this seed of David did evil in the sight of the Lord by walking in the way of the kings of Israel, but the actual cause was also revealed: *"...for the daughter of Ahab was his wife..."* (II Kings 8:18) It was also made known that his reign was patterned after the house of Ahab and *"Yet the LORD would not destroy Judah for David his servant's sake, as he promised him to give him always a light, and to his children."* (II Kings 8:19). His reign was suddenly cut short after eight years on the throne. It is only God that can repair faulty foundations and it is unto Him we should commit our cause.

There are several destinies to be examined in this and the next two chapters. We shall look at both the Bible and practical human examples of those who live amongst us. This is to help us relate to the issues raised and be able to effect change.

1. Truncated Destiny

In Job 5:3 we read an account that gives us a glimpse of what truncated destiny is all about: *"I have seen the foolish taking root: but suddenly I cursed his habitation."* This is the picture of hope rising and hope suddenly dashed. Imagine a person who a couple of years ago graduated from college, secured a well paying job and looks forward to bright future ahead but suddenly sleeps one night and never wakes up the next morning. He had secured a future and built upon it before the enemy came to terminate his race of life. There are several bright futures like the one described in both marked and unmarked graves as we speak. It was not their desire to bow out, if they were given the choice they would have chosen to live but their root was cursed and the hand of the wicked one truncated their destinies.

I also recall the story of a young man who had labored rigorously for several years to secure the United States of America travel visa but to no avail until luck smiled on him. He got the visa made the necessary travel arrangements, boarded an airplane from Lagos, Nigeria and arrived New York only to be shot by a homeless drug addict over a request for a dollar. He was too excited to note the aura of desperation in the voice of his assailant – only if he had known that area boys on this side of the world have access to guns ten times over compared to where he was coming from, he probably would have been much cautious. Because he failed to watch his back the enemy shot him and stole away with his wallet. His dream of coming to live in God's own country was suddenly truncated. What a pity!

Why is the person referred to in the passage of scriptures under examination called foolish? It is because the foolish man does not retain God in his heart neither does he call on him in trouble. *"The wicked, through the pride of his countenance, will not seek after God: God is not in all his thoughts."* (Ps 10:4). The foolish does his own thing and has explanation for every storm around him. He believes he is self sufficient and does not need God. He has everything worked out but what he fails to note is that living independent of God is surrendering to the dominion of evil forces. And as we well know – *"..the tender mercies of the wicked are cruel."* (Pro 12:10)

The fool just began the race of life and while things are just taking shape, he suddenly falls down and dies. This does not happen without warnings as situations like these always assume a particular or peculiar pattern. But because the fool lacks the temerity to seek God and find a way out of the mess he finds himself he never cries for help but only explain his situations away. This is also one reason the Bible refers to them as hypocrites in heart: *"But the hypocrites in heart heap up wrath: they cry not when he bindeth them. They die in youth, and their life is among the unclean.* (Job 36:13)

The foolish is a loser because of the consequences of his actions he is not spared. Yet the God we serve is a God of mercy who is willing to forgive our sins and deliver us from the mountains higher than us. It is His utmost desire to set the captives free and bring them to the place of peace and rest, but the fool will not cry. The challenges of life ought to have been solved only if we have yielded to his saving grace and trusted in His mercy. Job 36 reiterates the benefits that the foolish man ought to have enjoyed if only he had cried for help:

"He delivereth the poor in his affliction, and openeth their ears in oppression. Even so would he have removed thee out of the strait into a broad place, where there is no straitness; and that which should be set on thy table should be full of fatness. But thou hast fulfilled the judgment of the wicked: judgment and justice take hold on thee." (Job 36:14-17)

If action truly speaks louder than words we can safely declare that the foolish man by his denial and inaction is saying there is no God. *"The fool hath said in his heart, There is no God. They are corrupt, they have done abominable works, there is none that doeth good."* (Ps 14:1). The products of their thoughts are the filth, corruption and disaster that follow them. Their abominable works procure for them judgment and destruction. And in time of trouble they have no helper. *"...neither is there any to deliver them."* (Job 5:4).

A good example from the Bible can be found in Matthew 22:25-27 where we see a family of seven brothers truncated in life. *"Now there were with us seven brethren: and the first, when he had married a wife, deceased, and, having no issue, left his wife unto his brother:*

Likewise the second also, and the third, unto the seventh. And last of all the woman died also."

The above is a pathetic case of a family destroyed without any helper. Seven sons in a row died without leaving any seed behind and last of all, the woman herself died. Truncated destiny is real and it is energized by the spirit of impossibility. The spirit makes it impossible to reach one's goal. It is a dream killer.

There was also a sister who in her prime enjoyed the single privilege of having 32 brothers proposed to her and never did she at the end of the day walk through the aisle with any one of them. Her desperation to secure the hands of other men in marital overtures thereafter never yielded any fruit. The dream killer truncated this destiny till she gave up the fight and resigned to fate.

What is the summary of the matter? The Bible tells us in Psalm 5:5-8 in a succinct comment, declaration and prayer that:

"The foolish shall not stand in thy sight: thou hatest all workers of iniquity. Thou shalt destroy them that speak leasing: the LORD will abhor the bloody and deceitful man. But as for me, I will come into thy house in the multitude of thy mercy: and in thy fear will I worship toward thy holy temple. Lead me, O LORD, in thy righteousness because of mine enemies; make thy way straight before my face."

2. Vandalized Destiny

A vandalized destiny is a future being hopelessly messed up in the very eyes of its owner and the person could do nothing about it. It is the story of one subjected to plunder because of captivity. This person is a product of terrible foundation, and is under the strong influences of ordinances and covenants ruling his or her life with impunity.

Just like truncated destiny these ones in time of trouble have no helper. Their harvest is eaten up by the hungry and robbers take away their substance and all they had ever labored for in life: *"His children are far from safety, and they are crushed in the gate, neither is there any to deliver them. Whose harvest the hungry eateth up, and*

taketh it even out of the thorns, and the robber swalloweth up their substance." (Job 5:4-5)

Samson, a study in destiny vandalized, is a very good example.

How did we meet Samson? This is significant if we must understand this subject. After the encounter with the angel, Manoah's wife conceived and gave birth to a son they named Samson: **"....and the child grew, and the LORD blessed him"** (Judges 13:24). He was so blessed, endowed and empowered that the Bible confirms that **",,,the Spirit of the LORD began to move him at times in the camp of Dan between Zorah and Eshtaol."** V25

But unfortunately, this move of the spirit was not sustained by righteous living. What went wrong here? We could safely deduce that it was his foundation. One, he had a father, Manoah, who was not in control enough to be as Abraham who taught his household how to keep the way of the Lord, and do justice and judgment (Gen 18:19). His wife was the one in charge and the sustainer of the direction of the home. Manoah was a restless man who was not diligent enough concerning spiritual matters. He could easily compete for the trophy of Esau who despised spiritual things, and sought thereafter for it in tears (Heb 12:16-17).

Twice this man missed the angel who brought the message of blessing to his household. He was not where the object of his peace and blessing was resident even when he prayed for the opportunity to repeat itself the second time, he was still not there. God answered his prayer for divine visitation, the angel that brought the message showed up but for the intervention of his wife he would have lost out (Judges 13:1-5). The encounter reveals his spiritual shallowness and lack of spiritual understanding when he believed and insisted they were going to die because they saw an angel: **"And Manoah said unto his wife, We shall surely die, because we have seen God."** (Judges 13:22)

Thank God for the spiritual insight of his wife who began to reason with him that God would not have accepted their offering, bring such a message of hope and then later kill them (v23). The level of Manoah's spirituality could best be compared with that of Elkannah, whose wife

Hannah, singlehandedly prayed, named and nurtured the child Samuel. Of course, we are aware of the consequence. Even though through the help of the Holy Spirit, Samuel grew up to be a man who fulfilled God's purposes in his ministry yet he was imbalanced in the training of his children to the point in which the nation rejected them.

"And it came to pass, when Samuel was old, that he made his sons judges over Israel. Now the name of his firstborn was Joel; and the name of his second, Abiah: they were judges in Beersheba. And his sons walked not in his ways, but turned aside after lucre, and took bribes, and perverted judgment. Then all the elders of Israel gathered themselves together, and came to Samuel unto Ramah, And said unto him, Behold, thou art old, and thy sons walk not in thy ways: now make us a king to judge us like all the nations. But the thing displeased Samuel, when they said, Give us a king to judge us." (I Samuel 8:1-6)

How was this vacuum created? Samuel suffered lack of father figure in his life when he was growing up. Elkannah was not there to nurture him to manhood and also teach him how to raise a child. Unfortunately for Samuel, he grew up early in life under the tutelage of a spiritual leader, Eli who was not better. This is because the Bible intimated us with the sons of Eli who were referred to as *"...sons of Belial, they knew not God"* (I Sam 2:12). He was practically underdeveloped in this area.

With this background, it is therefore clear and understandable why Samson turned out be who he was. He was a spoilt child, who got whatever he wanted. It was no wonder that he was introduced in Judges 14:1-20 where *"..he saw a woman in Timnath..."* The next we heard of him was that he was with a harlot in Gaza (Judges 16:1-3) and finally with Delilah in the valley of Sorek where his fate was sealed (Judges 16:4-31). His case never ceased to amaze me. He was never satisfied with one woman and placed his destiny in the hands of fair weather women till he was fatally vandalized:

"And when Delilah saw that he had told her all his heart, she sent and called for the lords of the Philistines, saying, Come up this once, for he hath shewed me all his heart. Then the lords of the Philistines came up unto her, and brought money in their hand. And she made

him sleep upon her knees; and she called for a man, and she caused him to shave off the seven locks of his head; and she began to afflict him, and his strength went from him. And she said, The Philistines be upon thee, Samson. And he awoke out of his sleep, and said, I will go out as at other times before, and shake myself. And he wist not that the LORD was departed from him. But the Philistines took him, and put out his eyes, and brought him down to Gaza, and bound him with fetters of brass; and he did grind in the prison house." (Judges 16:18-21)

He lay on the laps of a woman who tricked him to get hold of the source of his strength and thereafter toyed with his destiny. Just for a few minutes of pleasure he sacrificed a glorious future and allowed the flesh to terminate a rich destiny. His vision was marred as his eyes were gorged out, and he became an object of ridicule in the camp of the Philistines. A once notable hero was now reduced to zero. Not only did they vandalize his virtues he was also reduced in value.

Many articulate appointed and anointed young men and women have fallen into the same path because of the pleasures of the moment. For some, it is power, money and women, while several anointed women also have being derailed by men too. And others it was just the position of power they suddenly found themselves that destroyed them. In the process they abused privileges, stepped on toes, disregarded authorities and despised old age/wisdom and ran into the very belly of hell. They are only remembered if the evil account of their deeds is mentioned. But we thank God who always because of His loving-kindness gives men a second chance. We see this in the case of Samson: *"Howbeit the hair of his head began to grow again after he was shaven."v22*

To the glory of God, whoever you are and wherever you may be the God of second chance would cause your hair to grow again. He will restore your former glory and give you hope to face the future again. Do not lose hope, but only look up your redeemer is nigh thee. Samson's strength returned, but in their foolishness nemesis was about to catch up with them. God was about to avenge the eyes of his servant and redeem his image hence the Lord of the Philistines made a foolish request.

"And it came to pass, when their hearts were merry, that they said, Call for Samson, that he may make us sport. And they called for Samson out of the prison house; and he made them sport: and they set him between the pillars." v25

In their warped minds they forgot as they rejoiced over their sworn enemy, Samson that the sole reason they were able to apprehend him was because his hair was shaven. It never occurred to any of them not even Delilah, whom I presume might be there to enjoy the glory of being the instrument used to overcome the enemy and the pleasure that this glory attracted, that his hair had started to grow again. God affected their memory and wiped away their thinking faculty to the degree that while he was making sport not a single person recall the ability of this man and asked that they took precautionary measures. They paid dearly for their carelessness and lack of caution. Samson took advantage of the moment and did what was best in the circumstance – securing an opportunity to punish his captors:

"And Samson said unto the lad that held him by the hand, Suffer me that I may feel the pillars whereupon the house standeth, that I may lean upon them. Now the house was full of men and women; and all the lords of the Philistines were there; and there were upon the roof about three thousand men and women, that beheld while Samson made sport." V26-27

Not only did Samson do this, he prayed to the Almighty God, the giver of life and strength to intervene for him as he proceeded in his game plan. Whatever is committed to God in prayer receives the assuring presence of the Lord and God as He has promised to always answer prayer. It may not be the way you want but He does answer prayer. So, Samson in this solemn moment said:

"O Lord God, remember me, I pray thee, and strengthen me, I pray thee, only this once, O God, that I may be at once avenged of the Philistines for my two eyes. And Samson took hold of the two middle pillars upon which the house stood, and on which it was borne up, of the one with his right hand, and of the other with his left.... And he bowed himself with all his might; and the house fell upon the lords, and upon all the people that were therein. So the dead which

**he slew at his death were more than they which he slew in his life."
V28-30**

The painful thing however was his final foolish prayer request: *"…
And Samson said, Let me die with the Philistines." v30* He did not
need to have died with them. He lost hope with life and desired death
when God could have given him life in the midst of his affliction. The
same God that caused water to come out of a jawbone when Samson
was thirsty after having wrought a great victory over the Philistines
could have helped him overcome his enemy and still lived. He found
his way back to the God of second chance, in spite of his condition he
remembered God's loving-kindness and his plenteous mercies, repented
and cried for help. The Lord who was willing to help him out of his
bad situation helped him to kill more in his death than in his life time.
(v30)

The intervention of God when Samson prayed, reminds me of a jinxed
house occupied by four professors living close to a university community.
Three of them had lost the use of their cars to inexplicable malfunctioning
parts, and were therefore forced to park them because of the continuous
drain on their finances as no welcome solutions were found to repair
them. The fourth lecturer who had his own car still running did so
with a lot of faith and prayer fireworks. He was confronted with a lot
of challenges such as missing accidents narrowly, inexplicable engine
hiccups and delays as he ran the car with desperation. Even, though
he was headed in the direction of the first three, this was not going to
happen without a fight.

In his desperation he set a prayer watch over the matter and made a
desperate cry to God. He was aware of the similarity of his predicament
with that of his colleagues who were forced to park their cars.
Consequently, they were all at his mercies as they all had to cramp
inside his small car to go to work. However, in the course of his one-
man-fiery prayers that span seven days of vigil, the Lord in the early
hour of the morning of the seventh day spoke to him. He told him to
stop praying that he was ready to reveal the secret behind his and their
problems. He was instructed to take his torch and proceed to the back
of the house.

On getting there, the Lord ministered to him to open the lid covering the potable well from which the households draw water. He did and introduced the light of a torch inside the well. As soon as he did he noticed something moving inside the well. The Lord then told him to throw in a bucket and to attempt to pull the moving object out of the well. After several attempts his effort was fruitful and he pulled the unknown object out of the well. Lo and behold it was a tortoise!

Tortoise is one of the many animals used to raise a formidable altar of witchcraft afflictions against innocent and ignorant folks. He noticed on dropping the bucket that the tortoise had four necklaces with name tags on its neck. He realized on close examination as the restless animal struggled to escape, that the four name tags on its neck were that of his three other colleagues and his. At this point he screamed and burst into sporadic prayer in the spirit. He was a mixed bag of anger and anxiety. When he came to himself he went after the tortoise that was frantically struggling inside the bucket to escape nemesis. He picked a big stone nearby and began to crack its shell until he broke its head while still praying in tongues.

Having paralyzed and demobilized this evil being, he thereafter went inside his apartment to get a bottle of paraffin oil, poured it on the dead tortoise and roasted it to near ashes. He continued burning it until it became unrecognizable. Less than an hour thirty minutes into his breakthrough, his landlord who had felt the spiritual impact of the divine release and encounter showed up at his doorstep. The encounter that ensued was not the kind you want to experience during the early hour of the day. The man spoke in parables and told the tenant that he knew what he had done and that he would hear from him. This was a challenge to spiritual context but guess who prevailed at the end of the day? It was the tenant who had the God of heaven as his protector.

The four tenants in the house were free from witchcraft affliction and were eternally grateful to the Lord. These vandalized destinies recovered strength because there was one man amongst them who refused to allow the wicked to continue to plunder them. He fought the devil to a standstill and took the kingdom by force. That is what God has called us to do to the enemy of our souls.

3. Snuffed out Destiny

The operation of snuffed out destiny always results in tragic end. It sometimes manifests on a large scale cutting across geographical areas of land, multiple car accidents, plane crashes and civil unrest that snuff out the lives of the best and brightest. In my home country, Nigeria I have read about cases of student unrest and subsequent violent encounters with law enforcement agencies that resulted in the death of innocent ones who never participated in the riot. A particular case in point was the untimely death of a final year law student of a University in Nigeria who, during one of such riots, was cut down in his prime by the stray bullets of law enforcement agents on his way from the library. Here was a rising star or a shining light suddenly snuffed out. Job Chapter 5 verse 4 captures the graphic picture of what this is all about thus: ***"His children are far from safety, and they are crushed in the gate, neither is there any to deliver them."***

The sad thing as mentioned earlier is that it always ends in untimely death. A good example as we examine the Bible further is in the gospel of Mathew Chapter 2 where we see the account of some wise men that followed the star of Jesus to the palace of Herod. He refused to show his surprise but wisely welcomed them and told them to return to tell him when they found the new born king. However, they never did having received divine instruction to the contrary from the Lord (Mt 2:8-12).

When Herod discovered that they stood him up, he was terribly infuriated and he ordered the cold blooded murder of innocent children from 0-2years:

"Then Herod, when he saw that he was mocked of the wise men, was exceeding wroth, and sent forth, and slew all the children that were in Bethlehem, and in all the coasts thereof, from two years old and under, according to the time which he had diligently inquired of the wise men. Then was fulfilled that which was spoken by Jeremiah the prophet, saying, In Rama was there a voice heard, lamentation, and weeping, and great mourning, Rachel weeping for her children, and would not be comforted, because they are not." (Matt 2:16-18)

The Bible tagged it as the cry of Rachel, in Rama for her children, and would not be comforted for they were not. Their lives were simply snuffed out in untimely death. While the book of Proverbs in the New Living Translation of the Bible gives us the following rendition which refers solely to the portion of the wicked, it is pathetic to mention that some unfortunate folks have found themselves in this category and their lives have been snuffed out before their time:

"The life of the godly is full of light and joy, but the light of the wicked will be snuffed out." (Prov. 13:9)

"If you insult your father or mother, your light will be snuffed out in total darkness." (Prov. 20:20)

I recall the painful story of a family who their grandmother relocated with her grandsons from one of the cities to Dallas after the inexplicable untimely deaths of her sons and grandson. The 19 year old son of this family was shot at a gas station in a similar circumstance that his brother was shot five days away from the time of his death two years earlier. They were both killed by stray bullets from the guns of armed robbers trying to rob gas stations. The grandmother could not unravel why her sons were being killed for no just cause yet the book of Job gives us the clue that the: *"...children are far from safety, and they are crushed in the gate, neither is there any to deliver them."* (Job 5:4)

4. Abused Destiny

This is a pathetic case of laboring in vain without having anything to show for one's effort. Those who suffer under the captivity of Abused Destiny fit the phrase that literarily translates as: Monkey does the work, but Baboon reaps the proceeds. This clearly sheds light on the key verse of this subject which reads: *"Whose harvest the hungry eateth up, and even taketh it out of the thorns, and the robber swallowed up their substance"* (Job 5:5).

Those involved in this affliction sometimes are hardworking, intellectually endowed and committed personalities who fate had not allowed to succeed in life. They find themselves in circumstances that seem to be beyond their power and every attempt to break through robs them of their personhood. It is as if they do not have what it takes to make it in life, yet they put in their best but are never given the commensurate rewards. They are used, abused and left with almost nothing to show for their grandeur efforts.

I have witnessed a lot of abuses in this part of the world where God had brought me to make my home. Even though you possess the best of education, left a good paying job and have what it takes to excel yet as soon as you arrive the shores of this nation you have to know your way very well or else you would have to begin again.

You face the first challenge of your academic laurels not matching what obtains here even if you studied in the UK not to talk of Africa! The challenges of language (accent & diction), culture, tradition and social demands/work ethics as required within the system stare you in the face. You sometimes feel like a fish out of water when you encounter any of these challenges. There are Transcript Evaluation Agencies that could interpret the degrees brought from Africa and other parts of the world. The interpreted results could be used to do either retraining or proceed to career path that enhances ones dignity. However, in some cases the contrary is the case. Like someone hinted, it is the family or people you encounter as you come in that determine your future path especially if you are not strong willed. For example, if the circle of people you first meet are professional cab drivers the chances are that you will end up becoming one no matter your qualifications.

For example there are many with two Masters Degrees who have had to swallow their pride and return to do a degree program less than Bachelors (Associate Degree) in nursing (LVN for that matter!). Some even found themselves beginning at the lowest rung of the ladder - Certified Nurse Aid (CNA) because they were wrongly counseled. While there is nothing wrong with starting out at the lowest rung of the ladder, what is wrong is to remain there forever. It could be a starting point but not a permanent vocation for someone who had earned a degree in any part of the world. While some through divine intervention survive the setback and move on, some have not even been able to recover from the shock. Hence, they remain on the comfort zone of making fast money till reality catches up with them.

For example, I worked in a facility shortly when I arrived Dallas, Texas and I was sharing with my fellow battered colleagues that if one year passed and they still found me there they should arrest me cut my legs and throw me out of the place because I did not belong there. One of them found it so funny that he called the other guys within earshot to come and hear my strange comment. He began his response to me by pointing at some of our colleagues who had said the same thing five, ten and thirteen years ago but were still there. To the glory of God I was on my eleventh month there when the Lord asked me to leave before he began to open other doors for me. God intervened for me because I dared to trust in his mercies, and holding on to His word of promise. Praise the Lord!

A very good biblical example is the story of Jacob as we read in Gen 31:41. He worked 14 years for Laban's two daughters and 6 years for his cattle and his wages were changed ten times. If not for divine intervention Jacob would have returned to his father's land empty handed. He was so abused that he had to fight his way out to victory. God intervened for him in order to regain lost grounds, by revealing to him the secret of mating some of the animals, in such a way that resulted in his having the strong and healthy ones. God also multiplied his herd in such a miraculous way because God wanted to avenge him of Laban's abuses.

In conclusion, abused destiny turns a strong man to a weakling, a brilliant man to look like a nonentity, a wise man to a fool and forces them to be a shadow of themselves. Where it becomes obvious is that those they coached were able to make success of their ventures. These are clear comparative evidences to show that some forces are at work against them. The same information they provided and failed, others used and succeeded. Then it becomes clear that it is beyond the ordinary – because *"We war not against flesh and blood, but against principalities and powers, and the rulers of the darkness of this world, against spiritual wickedness in high places."*

Chapter Five
Troubled Destinies II

"I was not in safety, neither had I rest, neither was I quiet; yet trouble came." Job 3:20

Introduction

Having examined truncated, vandalized, snuffed out and abused destinies in the previous chapter, it is time to review in this chapter and the next the other identified destiny issues as seen in the Bible and our daily experiences. The reason this becomes necessary is for every individual to have a do it yourself idea of what is going on. A lot of times we scan through destiny related problems without breaking it down to manageably recognized or identifiable proportions for those who are concerned to deal with.

This is the reason time has been taken out to identify and relate each of the issues with the Bible and current happenings in our lives. Therefore, a prayerful examination of each will enable anyone in any of the categories highlighted to know what he or she has to deal with and also how to go about it. Where it becomes absolutely difficult to go it alone, the person involved having possessed an idea of what is going on should be able to know when to call for the necessary help in that circumstance. There have been many who do not know what to do and failed to call for help until it is almost too late. For the believer and those who choose to turn to the Lord help is always by your doorstep. The next one to be examined amongst others as we press on is Roller Coaster Destiny aka kadesh Barnea or Going Round in Circles.

5. Roller Coaster Destiny.

Those who are under the affliction of destiny destroyer end up perishing out of restless frustration of wandering all over the place for no good reason. Many who suffer under the hold of this spirit find occupation in unproductive yet inexplicable restless gallivanting over the place. They move house, job, business, church and in the worst extreme marriage at the blink of an eye. They find unusual energy in fruitless mobility that has caused them to become "A rolling stone that gathers no Morse."

A critical examination of such situations in the lives of those concerned tends to reveal the abnormality of its occurrence and the frequency at which it also occurs. This without any doubt evinces a picture of someone acting out an unseen script with forceful alacrity or urgency that compels immediate action. They may not be able to explain why they do it because in many of the cases the end actually does not usually justify the means. It is always a strong or compelling feeling that I just have to move. No amount of counsel can be heeded at that point in time. Even though it is obvious to onlookers that the move is unnecessary yet they do it anyhow because of the controlling force of evil behind it. The sad news is that such merry go rounding always end up in poverty, loss of self esteem, hope and social support. It is always a story of beginning again.

I met a man many years ago who told me his pathetic story. He left Nigeria the place of his birth to Germany where he crossed over to Austria as an adventurous young man. While in his early twenties he found such comfort in moving from city to city but when he got married with two kids he slowed down a bit but the urge still came very strong. He was a successful Disc Jockey in Vienna, Austria and money was coming in until he made a dive for another move to another part of Europe, England. It was in London, England that he began to question his move this time. After six months of depleting his savings, with a wife, two children and another baby on the way reality began to dawn on him, yet he concluded that perhaps another move would put an end to his suffering.

It was then that a door of opportunity opened to him and he began to bounce back and was doing well. The Lord blessed them with a new baby and the family of five had everything to thank God for. However, because he had no relationship with God in any form whatsoever he neither was saved nor went to church hence there was no way to receive divine help. At the peak of his bouncing back, the enemy showed up again and the urge to move came up so strongly. Without consulting with his wife he bought five air line tickets and insisted on leaving for Lagos, Nigeria the next day. The wife pleaded, begged and did all she could to make him see reason, but he turned deaf ears.

He told me "We left London with nothing but a few belongings, cash and our passports. All my cars, electronic gadgets, furniture and other things of value were left in our apartment building intact and I blindly walked away from them. It was when we landed at the Muritala Mohammed International Airport that my eyes opened. He said for the first three days I wept bitterly because I could not go back as I was an illegal resident in England. If I put pen on paper to calculate my losses because of my incessant movements they could run into millions of Naira." (Naira is the currency of exchange in Nigeria).

The story of the man above clearly shows that a satanic pull was at work and the pull was for destruction. At the root of this pull or push is a curse at work. We can recall that in the Bible the Lord in his anger made a pronouncement concerning the fate of the children of Israel and ensured it came to pass to the very last person as we read in the book of Numbers 13:33:

"And your children shall wander in the wilderness forty years, and bear your whoredoms, until your carcases be wasted in the wilderness."

Furthermore, He terminated the destinies of the original people who came out of Egypt by making them to wander in the wilderness till they all perished as we see in Numbers 32:13: **"And the LORD'S anger was kindled against Israel, and he made them wander in the wilderness forty years, until all the generation, that had done evil in the sight of the LORD, was consumed."** Num 32:13

Just like God made these men to wander till they perished, agents of darkness are also capable of making men run such rat race till they end up totally frustrated and become suicidal or die mysteriously. There are stories of people who in order to settle down have married seven wives and all ended in divorce. There are those who have lived in ten cities within a space of five years! There are also those who have moved from one academic faculty to the other that on the last count they have traversed up to five faculties and at the end came out with no worthwhile degree.

A good Biblical example of a roller coaster, unstable as the wind guy was Manoah, Samson's father. He was never at places where good things happen. Good things always happen behind him, either before he got to a place or shortly after he left. Jude verse 13 refers to these people as *"wandering stars,"* while the book of Job makes us to understand their plight. They are the ones:

"Whose harvest the hungry eateth up, and taketh it even out of the thorns, and the robber swalloweth up their substance." (Job 5:5)

Because they are not available to watch over their substance the hungry eats it up and even have the audacity to remove it out of the thorns while robbers take turns to swallow up their substance. What a pity! Then what is left for them? Nothing but sorrow tears and blood.

The Christians among them are known as the "dead in Christ" because all forms of catalogues of woes trail them just because they refused to be steadfast, strong, resolute and make up their minds to stand up for the truth. They want things the easy way, if it is not happening they are on the move again. They are just restless and find it difficult to be still and know God. While it is obvious that they are under a controlling influence they try hard to explain it away. Hence they lose every opportunity to be helped.

Yet, it is by waiting that one can appreciate God's presence. That is the reason he ordained twelve to be with him (Mk 3:14), not to go and preach first as many assume. In Psalm 110:1-2 God had to tell the son to:

"...Sit thou at my right hand, until I make thine enemies thy footstool."

You just have to learn to sit before you walk, and walk before you stand to resist the enemy. The foundation for your walk with God is based on what you learnt while you sat at his feet. These would be the raw materials for your walk with him. The equipment for your journey can be sourced at his feet, as you grow to know him more.

Even as you walk and stumble along you are not afraid because you have learnt that "He'll never leave you nor forsake you." Hence you are assured that he keeps his promise and jealously watches over his own. As you walk with him you receive strength to fight the enemy using:

".......the words of his grace that is able to build you up and give you an inheritance among those sanctified" (Acts 20:32).

As you do so, you are in the process of being able to submit first to God and then resist the devil (Jas 4:7) not the other way round.

Back to Manoah, we understand from Judges 13:6-14 that the angel of God brought a destiny impacting message to the family of this man and he was not there. But thank God for his rugged and determined wife who ran to fetch him and told him about the angel. There he immediately lifted up his voice in prayer and asked the God of mercy to send back the angel so that he might know how to handle the message sent. To the glory of God, the angel returned but lo and behold Manoah was not there:

"And the woman made haste, and ran, and shewed her husband, and said unto him, Behold, the man hath appeared unto me, that came unto me the other day. And Manoah arose, and went after his wife, and came to the man, and said unto him, Art thou the man that spakest unto the woman? And he said, I am. And Manoah said, Now let thy words come to pass. How shall we order the child, and how shall we do unto him? And the angel of the LORD said unto Manoah, Of all that I said unto the woman let her beware." (Judg. 13:10-13)

We thank God for his wife who refused to give up but pressed on to empower her husband. She could have done this a hundred times if she needed to. Neither did we see her take the position of leadership by telling the angel "You know what my husband is a useless blockhead, tell me what we need to know and I would take care of it." She was a woman of wisdom and honor, who was willing to defer to him in spite of his obvious weakness. At the end of the day through her resilience, she got him to meet the angel and the deal was sealed. But remember she had to persuade the angel to spare more time while she went to get him and not with a single complaint to him about what she had to go through to get him thereafter.

As mentioned earlier, the foundation of restless, roaming about spirit in Samson could be traced to his father. He was just running around in circles after one woman or the other until he got caught in the web of destruction that eventually suffocated him. Twice this man was enticed by his women to tell them his secrets: first the woman of Timnath whom he told his riddle (Judges 14:16-17) and Delilah (Judges 16:16-18). He seemed to have a terrible weakness not being able to resist external pressures from women.

Samson was a wonder who wandered about in frivolity. The book of Jude verse 13 gives us a caption on this kind of behavior: *"Raging waves of the sea, foaming out their own shame; <u>wandering stars,</u> to whom is reserved the blackness of darkness for ever."*

They are stars in their own rights but they are stars that wander about. God has made them to be wonders yet they choose to be wanderers who have the potential of drifting away from the truth. The truth is they:

".. wander out of the way of understanding..."

and therefore:

".. remain in the congregation of the dead." (Prov. 21:16),

This is nothing but signing in for perdition. May God send them quick help!

6. Stagnated Destiny

When a person at significant stages in life is not manifesting commensurate growth, it is safe to assume that stagnation has set in. Several lives have remained rooted to the spot because certain forces are at work to limit them from moving forward. There are situations that have kept men out of desired progress and succeeded in killing their will and aspiration. These individuals, bless their hearts, have done all they know to do but have not seen the needed result because the root of the matter has not been touched.

These ones work like an elephant and eat like an ant. These ones for any reason could not be labeled as lazy because they put in more hours than any of their colleagues or contemporaries dead or alive! What others do and get easy victory is always saddled with tales of woes if they ever venture there. Many of their rejected efforts have been applauded when done by others in their class. Many who know how hard working they are and see that their efforts do not produce expected results have a load of sympathy for them, yet could not do anything to change their situation. The best they could do is to put in a strong word of appeal on their behalf, which most of the times fall on deaf ears.

A typical example of stagnation in the Bible is the story of Jacob who served Laban for twenty years. Let us hear the account of the stagnation from the horses' mouth:

"Thus have I been twenty years in thy house; I served thee fourteen years for thy two daughters, and six years for thy cattle: and thou hast changed my wages ten times."

If not for the intervention of God Jacob, would have gone to his father's house empty handed.

The story that readily comes to my mind is that of two friends who graduated from high school and both shared a room each in a block of apartments. While one of them left after a few years to college the other took a government job. After twenty years the one who went to college saw the other at the bus station and stopped to talk with him. The other fellow was so excited to see his friend in a brand new car. Out of excitement he asked him whether that was his boss's car or his. His friend told him no, that it was one of his cars and went on to tell him that he lived in his own home he recently built.

The other guy wanting to equally sound impressive and match his friends' resume told him he had not done badly too because he had now moved to occupy the second room he was sharing with him twenty years before. He also told him he had been promoted two steps ahead in the civil service and rides a Honda 90 motorbike. If in twenty years all the progress you can make is to move from one room to two and have a few change to show as salary increase and a motorbike there is a problem!

Some of the people who are stagnated are sometimes complacent and satisfied with little. In spite of their potentials they resign to fate and leave life to chance and their familiar phrase is always "Whatever would be would be." This is the lie of the devil. Except a man works out his salvation with fear and trembling, his destiny could be terminated. There are many unfulfilled dreams in the grave yard. It is the diligent that cry to God, who watch him turn situations around in their favor.

Those who leave their lives to chance will not go too far. We must fight for every progress we make in order to be in control. No wonder the Bible charges us to subdue the earth. Failure to forcefully enforce divine mandate has caused many a great deal of pain. They lost control and were limited in life. Stagnation is an enemy of progress! God wants us to move forward.

7   Manipulated Destiny

This is a case of evil intervention in the path of a person's destiny. This manipulative intervention is either physical or spiritual in their execution. Those who do it are dream killers, faith quenchers and destiny terminators and they do it mostly out of envy, greed and covetousness. Their sole intent is to make sure you never arrive at the port of destiny. What gives them impetus is the fact that they are privy to certain enviable blessings that either have been pronounced over your life or is already showing signs of manifestation or the one you have shared with them that is in process. Just like Joseph's brothers they say:

"...Behold the dreamer cometh. Come now therefore, and let us slay him, and cast him into some pit, and we will say, Some evil beast hath devoured him: and we shall see what will become of his dreams." (Gen 37:19-20)

Their main goal was to manipulate his dreams by physically and forcefully diverting its course to their own advantage.

Even though Joseph was eventually sold as a slave to Potiphar's house, yet the Bible tells us God was with him. Initially it looked very much that his destiny was terminated, because he went down from being a beloved child to the house of enslavement. In spite of all he went through in the path of destiny, he broke through in Potiphar's house where he became the Overseer of all Potiphar's assets. This man learnt a lot in the house of Potiphar to make him an able administrator, strategist and shrewd business man. However because his time was up there, a destiny catalyst in the person of Potiphar's wife, unknowingly moved in to accelerate his move to the next level.

At the time it happened it was as if he was going further down into perdition, especially when you think his freedom had been taken from him, and was moved further away from fulfilling his dream yet God was at work. The way up with God is down and the situation that presents itself as being down is actually a bigger opportunity to go up when compared with the former.

There in the prison the path to Joseph's destiny began to blossom. He met several government officials whom he ministered to and was also involved with high caliber ministry oversight that affected some of these men. When the day of his remembrance came it was one of them that God used to speak to Pharaoh and made it possible for Joseph to stand before him and fulfill his dream. This appearance or experience ended a tough journey into the fulfillment of a dream nurtured from childhood, and began the journey to stardom. This confirms the fact that they can only delay your rise but they cannot stop it.

In another instance, destiny can be manipulated through deception of convincing your destiny helper that you are not whom he thought you were e.g. Ziba versus Mephibosheth. After the young man Mephibosheth was delivered from the horrors of Lodeba, the island of social confinement and relegation, he was restored to royalty as one of the princes who should eat on the kings table. Here was actually supposed to be his place but fate did not play in his favor for many years until David asked:

"Is there not yet any of the house of Saul, that I may show the kindness of God to him?" (II Sam 9:3).

Thereafter, the man Ziba came into the picture and he gave David Mephibosheth's information and that was it.

Shortly after his restoration, Absalom planned a coup that ousted David his father. Many of David's friends were on ground to see him off and express their loyalty to him. Ziba took advantage of the moment, and the handicap condition of Mephibosheth, and went to see David off while he left the lame man in the cold refusing to saddle him an ass. When David asked of him Ziba the schemer lied and he said he told me he was not interested in coming because he said now is the time for me to claim back the throne of my father. David then made a pronouncement that all the properties he restored to Mephibosheth should be shared with Ziba fifty-fifty. What a dangerous schemer Ziba was!

While we are at it I remember a testimony of a family of five sons who were faced with the challenge of barrenness. The first, second, third and fourth son all married but no children. The fifth was in the process of getting married, and while in the course of preparatory prayer he asked his fiancé what he noticed about his family. She responded without wasting anytime and thanked him for asking because the scandalous air of barrenness that hit the family seemed to be the talk of their small community and she was deadly afraid that she could be one of the statistics. While they took the matter to God, he counseled them to proceed on 21 days fast which they promptly obeyed.

On the 21st day of the fast the Lord told them not to receive handshake from anybody on the wedding day. Both husband and wife obeyed the divine instruction until a challenger came. She made a ring round the brother looking for an opportunity to disentangle his locked hands but he refused until someone came to his rescue. The woman then told them she was only trying to give him a handshake, to which she was told handshake was supposed to be a voluntary act and not by force. Therefore she should live the couple alone!

While she reluctantly left, the Lord ministered to His son and told him that was the destiny manipulator in the family. She was a blocker of the womb and every good thing that ought to have happened in the family. Both husband and wife thereafter at night knelt down before the faithful God and gave Him thanks. Within a space of three months the lady got pregnant. It elicited curious but envious wave of gossip that spread like wild fire in the small community where they lived.

The nosy eyes and steps that trailed her every movement each time she was out of her home gave her goose bumps. The fact that she knew they were not only watching her but also gossiping about whether the pregnancy was made up was strong in her mind. Various versions of speculative thoughts had filtered to her and her husband through some of their friends yet they put their trust in God.

The height of it was when the parents of the husband and his brothers wondered how they made it noting very well that they were believers just like them. He simply told them his victory was basically the result of diligent and desperate cry to Lord to deliver him and his wife from the problem of barrenness in his family. He told them how the Lord led them to have 21 days fast, the instruction not to shake hands and how God delivered them from the destiny terminator. They all realized that only if they had cried hard enough perhaps the Lord could have delivered them from the hole they have found themselves.

8. Delayed Destiny

While stagnated destiny remains on the spot until divine intervention moves the victim forward, delayed destiny gives the victim a measure of progress that is delayed in many ways. Delayed blessing is a pattern that reveals itself in achieving milestone goals at later time in life. What others achieve at 20 some arrive there at 30 or 35. For example, there is a family where down the family line the earliest time any member of the family gets married is 40 years old. This resulted in female members of the family to have between one and two children due to old age. There was one who got married at 50. That she had a child itself was as a result of miracle. Nothing seems to have changed in the stories of Daddy, Uncles, Aunties and cousins

Delayed destiny manifests across various spheres of life. There was a man who spent 13 years in medical school and because he could not make it, he had to be asked to leave with a 4 year degree certificate in Health sciences. Some suffer delayed promotion as well just like a woman who was on one salary scale for ten years until God intervened for her. For some it is in building projects, handling major assignments or task which by all facts on ground should not take long but one thing would follow after the other that they would need to call for prayer help to disentangle them from the crisis in their hands.

A readily available biblical example is the story of the man Terah, the father of Abraham. In fact his name means delay and he answered the consequences fully, that it affected four generations of his children as well as himself. We see clearly in Genesis how Abraham, Sarah, Isaac, Rebekah, Leah and Rachel suffered one form of delay or the other. While that of Rachel was glaring that of Leah was not that obvious until the Bible tells us in Genesis 29:31:

"And when the LORD saw that Leah was hated, he opened her womb: but Rachel was barren."

Why did God have to open her womb, if it was not shut, just like he did for Rachel?

"And God remembered Rachel, and God hearkened to her, and opened her womb." (Gen 30:22)

Another example of delay in the Bible is the story of Methuselah who lived 969 years and did not do much for God except that he was a baby factory. He was the son of a man who walked with God, and was not because God took him. His father Enoch had laid a foundation for divine precedence which he could have chosen to follow. While the average age of delivery in his time was sixty-five years Methuselah's first son came at the age of 187 years old.

"And Methuselah lived an hundred eighty and seven years, and begat Lamech." Gen 5:25.

The delay in the life of this man was so palpable that it also affected his son Lamech. In his own case:

"Lamech lived an hundred eighty and two years, and begat a son:" Gen 5:28

Chapter Six
Troubled Destinies III

"Man that is born of a woman is of few days and full of trouble. He cometh forth like a flower, and is cut down: he fleeth also as a shadow, and continueth not." (Job 14:1-2)

Introduction

Many have prolonged their sufferings and lived in penury in the midst of plenty and the worst thing a victim may do is to explain the situation away. Some also who have faced the reality of the mater on ground, have lost every ground of hope yet hope does not make ashamed. Their constant refrain have always been "The Lord will do it" How long shall we remain by the mountain side when it is obvious that the glory of God had departed from there?

The wise thing to do is to locate where the cloud of glory is moving and pursue it aggressively. Confront the issues of your life with desperate passion and do not look on while your destiny is being destroyed. *"The righteous cry and the Lord heareth, and delivereth them out of all their troubles"* (Psalm 34:17). Therefore cry out! Do not leave the matter of your life to chance. Rise up and do something about it, the Lord will take over from there. Be wise.

And for those whose constant philosophical statement is: **"The Lord will do it."** I have good news for you. It is time for you to know that you are not current because *"The Lord has done it"* and the following scriptures confirm it: *"I will praise thee for ever, because thou hast done it:."* (Ps. 52:9)

"Sing, O ye heavens; for the LORD hath done it:...." (Is. 44:23. So rise up and take the battle to the gate. Go after your lost possessions and recover all in the name of Jesus. You can do it in Jesus name!

With this knowledge clearly revealed to you, it is now your responsibility to discover and connect with what God has done. This is the reason why you need to know God for yourself. Many people today have second or third hand information about who God is and what he can do! This approach to life is not going to work for you. You need to experience God for yourself and it is for your own good. The book of Job 5:27 reiterates this fact: *"Lo this, we have searched it, so it is; hear it, and know thou it for thy good."*

The subjects we are dealing with are largely spiritual and cannot be handled with kid's glove. One needs to be diligent, steadfast and resilient as he pursues the goal for freedom. Good things do not come easy, just as freedom is costly- someone has to pay a price. Jesus did when he died on the cross and all the Holy Spirit is demanding from you is your deliberate pursuit of the goal to pay the price without looking back.

Be ready to pay the price and move to the next level. Do not look back no matter the obstacle you meet along the way. Do not be deterred: pray, fast, meditate and do warfare night and day until you get the result. Do not resign to fate but forcefully enforce the desire of God for your freedom by taking dominion even if you have to bring down the roof of where you are with violent cry.

Be encouraged help is on the way. Throw out your four anchors of hope: Love, Patience, Joy and Peace and as you pursue your goal with divine confidence in Him. You are assured of victory as you do so at the end of the day because hope does not put a man to shame. He is faithful!

"And patience, experience; and experience, hope: And hope maketh not ashamed; because the love of God is shed abroad in our hearts by the Holy Ghost which is given unto us." (Rom 5:4-5)

"For we are saved by hope: but hope that is seen is not hope: for what a man seeth, why doth he yet hope for? But if we hope for that we see not, then do we with patience wait for it." (Rom 8:24-25)

"Now the God of hope fill you with all joy and peace in believing, that ye may abound in hope, through the power of the Holy Ghost." (Rom 15:13)

With assured hope a man is empowered to do anything in God's name. As we continue our examination of this subject the next one to be considered amongst others is Frustrated Destiny.

9. Frustrated Destiny

A frustrated destiny is that which goes through inexplicable blockade in spite of obvious efforts put behind a given task. No matter how hard the man tries and keeps moving on, his hope is repeatedly dashed because of the power behind his case. It has been observed that such persons put in much effort, show unusual brilliance and have effected growth or change in the lives of others and what has worked for others through them is always frustrated when it comes to their turn. Everyone around them knows that the input does not justify the output and what they receive is not always commensurate with what they sacrificially labored for.

Why is the situation so? It is simply for them to throw in the towel and turn away from the path of destiny designed for them by God. It is an area where everyone observes that they have expertise yet things always go wrong and in such a bad way that it would draw shameful attention. This is to trigger a rethink about their acclaimed competence in the area of expertise they have been known to enjoy. As time passes those who have watched on the sideline begin to lose confidence in them as a result of repeated flip-flops in their output. Yet in the midst of their crisis, whosoever they assisted along the same line even with little efforts would enjoy enviable outputs. This then begins to draw the attention of those helped to the fact that an unseen hand is at work against the person's destiny as they could make obvious comparisons.

A good example is the story of one young dynamic fellow in a local assembly. This young man was so brilliant that he single handedly ran tutorial classes for teenagers in the church and the results were outstanding. All of them that sat for the West African School Leaving Certificate (WASC) did so well except he the coach. He did the exam that others did once and passed for four times and the results were F9 (or Fs) on all subjects. On the fifth year he resigned to fate and refused to register but decided to seek the face of the Lord concerning his troubling situation. It was while he waited that he got an unusual post office slip to go collect a registered mail from West African Examination Council (WAEC).

He rushed to the post office to get the package only to discover that he failed an examination he neither registered nor sat for. It was then he realized that there was a problem. He went straight to his pastor who organized a seven-day prayer and fasting retreat to get to the root of this ongoing problem. On the seventh day the Lord revealed to him that one of his father's wives was sitting over his text books. He thereafter visited the polygamous family of his father's five wives and several children in the village. He waited till 12.00 am to begin to do warfare and the time he finished in the morning he had commanded the fire of the Holy Spirit to roast the buttocks of whoever was sitting over his academic progress.

By 6.00 am in the morning he went to bed but woke up around 10.00 am when he made an unusual altar call. He lined up all his father's wives with their children as if he was observing a guard of honor mounted for him. As he paces to and fro in between them, looking to both his right and left, he told them he was going to sit for the next WASC and if he failed what they heard overnight would just be a sample. They were so terrified that they told him he would pass and in fact he did. His engagement in spiritual warfare broke through for him and the Lord was glorified.

The story of Haman in the book of Esther is also an interesting one. Here was a man who in spite of all his achievements in the nation was frustrated by the refusal of Mordecai to bow to him. Each time he saw him at the gate and experienced his recalcitrant attitude he felt terrible and wanted so much to get him out of the way. Yet, in spite of all the power he wielded in the nation he could not just touch the man without a good reason: - this was his frustration. He however sought counsel with his wife and friends as to what to do to remove this obstacle from his path. The advice they gave him led to the beginning of his rapid downfall. Needless to say if he had known that this was his path to destruction and final termination of his and his children's destiny he probably would not have followed it.

"Then said Zeresh his wife and all his friends unto him, Let a gallows be made of fifty cubits high, and to morrow speak thou unto the king that Mordecai may be hanged thereon: then go thou in merrily with the king unto the banquet. And the thing pleased Haman; and he caused the gallows to be made. (Est. 5:14)

As soon as the gallows was made God began a series of rapid moves to prepare Mordecai for the throne. The first was that the king was unable to sleep and hence he sent for the book of records where he discovered that Mordecai had not been rewarded for saving his life. While he began to think about what to do Haman was in the court and he was asked what should be done to the man whom the king wanted to honor. He gave the king an enviable list of what should be done to the person because in his egoistical thinking he thought he was the man but he was wrong.

"Then the king said to Haman, Make haste, and take the apparel and the horse, as thou hast said, and do even so to Mordecai the Jew, that sitteth at the king's gate: let nothing fail of all that thou hast spoken. (Est. 6:10)

After the parade the humiliation was too much for Haman that the Bible records that: "..*Haman hasted to his house mourning, and having his head covered....*" (Est. 6:12). It is true that pride comes before destruction. His thought earlier in the chapter to destroy the Jewish race because of one man is nothing different from what Adolf Hitler eventually did, but in his own case God frustrated him (Est. 3:5-15). God indeed: "..*frustrateth the tokens of the liars, and maketh diviners mad; that turneth wise men backward, and maketh their knowledge foolish;*" (Is 44:25).

His every effort to get at Mordecai failed and yet he kept going down. This was best captured by the words of his wife and friends who by their words prophetically nailed his coffin. *"....Then said his wise men and Zeresh his wife unto him, If Mordecai be of the seed of the Jews, before whom thou hast begun to fall, thou shalt not prevail against him, but shalt surely fall before him....*" (Est 6:14)

Exactly what they told him happened in matter of hours. While he was still lamenting his woes amongst his wife and friends the message came to call him to Esther's Banquet. He rushed out from the presence of his wife and friends to his utter destruction. Queen Esther who had rehearsed her lines properly threw the bombshell at the appropriate time when the king asked her what her petition was! Haman did not know what hit him when he heard what Esther had to say. He was so terrified and confused that in his attempt to plead with her for his life he fell over her across the bed. He acted in desperation because: "…. *he saw that there was evil determined against him by the king.*" (Est. 7:7)

The downfall of this man who had a rapid rise and descent from glory to grace was so dramatic that he never had the chance to rethink. The Lord removed the bowels of mercy that could have saved him and he had no helper. He was alone in his confusion that no one showed him pity. When the king returned and saw him lying across over her in bed in his attempt to plead for his life his king's reaction was swift. He said: "… *Will he force the queen also before me in the house? As the word went out of king's mouth, they covered Haman's face. And Harbonah, one of the chamberlains, said before the king, Behold also, the gallows fifty cubits high, which Haman had made for Mordecai, who spoken good for the king, standeth in the house of Haman. Then the king said, Hang him thereon. So they hanged Haman on the gallows that he had prepared for Mordecai. Then was the king's wrath pacified.*" (Est.7:8-10)

10. Stifled or Gagged Destiny

This is a situation where the person involved finds himself suffering from frequent loss of inspiration, focus or vision in such a way that a man who is gagged loses air. There are many things such persons are incapable of doing because they do not have the life that should sustain their desire. Just like the man who lacks sufficient airflow into his lungs is always tired or weak, these ones always lack the resolve to push or move on because they are weak.

Sometimes you see them pick strength when they have the opportunity to breath well and when you hope that this should be sustained they revert to status quo. One then begins to think perhaps they have no integrity or they are timid but a close look at the pattern reveals the root of their problem. There is a landlord who has kept his paws on their throat blocking the airways intermittently at will. When he releases them they function a while and when he wraps his hands around their throat they cease to function effectively.

It comes in different ways and has its root in witchcraft. You see a man full of life bubbling and doing fine as long as his mum or wife in some cases is not involved. The moment you mention either of their names an inexplicable fear grips him and he loses the ability to function. Sometimes you have a good deal with this person and everything is set and working well until he gets home to share it with his wife and then the story changes.

The same is true of a woman also as the problem cuts across sexes. The persons involved cannot take a simple one-on-one fair decision on their own except their partners sanction it. It does not matter whether the partner's decision is reasonable, unspiritual and hurtful or not he or she would abide by it trembling. You could see the fear of saying no and the consequences it will attract written all over them.

There is nothing wrong to give honor to your spouse or parent but a boundary should be drawn between controlling fear and healthy collaboration. When a man voices out his anxiety in a cry for understanding "I'll have loved to do this but for my wife, you know her!" He's telling you who is in charge. It goes for both sides as well. A man too can be so controlling to a point in which a woman is under his oppressive hold that the husband has become a terror to the household. The family is at peace only if the man is asleep or out of the home because he bawls and he has literally become a god to be worshipped by his family.

The other extreme is there is no obvious controlling person around the man but at a certain season or period he suddenly becomes fearful. The target of which it is to distract him and make him lose balance and mess things up at home, office or church. This in turn spoils his record of love, integrity, commitment and honesty. He turns out to be untrustworthy, unfaithful, sloppy and distracted and no one wants to take him serious because they have not come to understand the unseen hand at work over his life. He becomes impulsive, sometimes confused and confounded. This is the time the normally articulate and diligent person begins to major on minor against his will. During this time his unstable and miscalculated in-discretionary actions set many to thinking – what's going on here?

The man that readily comes to mind in the scriptures is Elkanah the husband of Peninnah and Hannah, the mother of Samuel. He was so much controlled that he lost the leadership of his home to Peninnah who on a regular basis found her natural pastime in tormenting Hannah concerning her childlessness. Even though a religious man who went to Shiloh every year, he was not able to teach his household judgment and justice. There was no indication of fairness in his conduct towards Hannah except that he always secured for her a worthy portion. Of what weight is that to a woman who was constantly emotionally battered by her household enemy – Peninah even in his presence without recourse for reconciliation? We see in this man, who was always trying to play safe, the inability to call Peninnah to order. He was by all means trying to eat his cake and have it and as well enjoy the goodness of both worlds.

While he gravitated towards Hannah whom he loved dearly, he could not contradict Peninnah the tormentor who held on to the rulership of the home with strong grip. As a result he relinquished the authority of his own household to the one who called the shots because she possessed the clear proof of her authority to claim the right of significance in the home – fruits of the womb. Hence, she became the willing adversary by choice, for so the Bible calls her: ***"And her adversary also provoked her sore, for to make her fret, because the LORD had shut up her womb."*** (I Sam 1:6)

I perceive that Elkannah sometimes was there while Peninnah tormented her and he could do nothing but keep quiet only to go later and console Hannah in the absence of Peninnah. When the eyes of this man eventually opened to the needs of his wife for emotional support, he bungled it by making a foolish and insensitive statement. He lost the good sense of knowing that nothing could replace the absence of a child in a woman's life not even the presence of a man. Yet in his ignorance he equated himself with ten sons – what a terrible thing to say?

"Then said Elkanah her husband to her, Hannah, why weepest thou? and why eatest thou not? and why is thy heart grieved? am not I better to thee than ten sons?" (v8)

This statement jolted Hannah to life and triggered her move towards breakthrough because it made her to realize she was alone in her search for a child, at least Peninnah had given him children and he had had enough not to worry about her childlessness: *"So Hannah rose up after they had eaten in Shiloh, and after they had drunk. Now Eli the priest sat upon a seat by a post of the temple of the LORD. And she was in bitterness of soul, and prayed unto the LORD, and wept sore.* (I Sam 1:9-10),

She was forced to face reality and carried her cross as she began a determined effort to achieve a breakthrough in spite of her husband's weakness. Not only did God answer her, she got the baby, did the naming and single handedly loaned the baby to God. The husband was like an on-looker in the transition process and the execution of the vow she made. He was not there as expected for Hannah at all because he was physically and spiritually gagged or stifled.

"And when she had weaned him, she took him up with her, with three bullocks, and one ephah of flour, and a bottle of wine, and brought him unto the house of the LORD in Shiloh: and the child was young." (I Sam 1:24)

The testimony that followed Hannah's action was not only inspiring but eye opening because it clearly affirmed the result of her walk with God. She had a need, mapped out her strategy to meet the need and paid the price to get it. Without any doubt God needed a priest and a virgin womb to carry it. Hannah was positioned to meet God's need and her own, because God saw in her a willing vessel ready to pay the price.

As it is always the case for those who God uses, it was not easy at first for Hannah who waited on pity party. God allowed a series of events that pushed her out of her comfort zone, and hence when she got it and made the move she was able to testify later after having paid the price in prayer that: *"For this child I prayed; and the LORD hath given me my petition which I asked of him:...."* (I Sam 1:27)

What a beautiful ending to a tortuous, winding and hurtful journey both in its process and execution. While it lasted Hannah was the pun in the hands of Peninnah, and it seems the period of pain was not going to end yet the Alpha and the Omega was there watching every move. Because He knows the end from the beginning and the beginning from the end, He is aware of where a matter will end therefore He keeps silent and watches us as we map out our path through the journey. Wherever and whenever we want to miss it He steps in to give direction even as we trust in him to do so. Oh what an awesome God He is! May His name be praised forever.

11. Unappreciated Destiny

This is a recurring decimal in some people's lives where they are neither appreciated nor recognized for the good they have done. No matter how serious their commitments and heavy their inputs might be nobody remembers them. This pattern trails them in many areas of their lives. They are most of the time misunderstood, misrepresented, undervalued, underrated and unappreciated at various levels of life. They do so much and are sold out to what they do, yet while others take the glory of their efforts they are always rewarded with disappointment and disgrace.

We see this trend at work in Joseph's life. Here was a man who had all things going for him in Portiphar's house. A trusted and committed servant who in the time of trouble all he had done in Portiphar's house were not taken into account at least to temper justice with mercy. He singlehandedly built the business empire of Portiphar. His contributions, efforts or inputs in building the house of Portiphar did not count because of unappreciated destiny at work in his life. When his trouble came, he was just treated as a nonentity, cast into prison as an insignificant object of use and ready to be discarded at its owner's whims and caprices.

Even when he got to prison, he was involved in managing the affairs of the place and touched many lives in the process. He was like the prison Chaplain even though he was an inmate himself. He provided pastoral care to those with issues that were beyond their spiritual understanding. He also provided reflections, encouragement and care to those hurting. In the process he found two officials of Pharaoh who had challenges with respect to their dreams. He interpreted each of the dreams to the dreamers and used the opportunity to ask to be remembered or appreciated in Gen 40:14: "*But think on me when it shall be well with thee, and shew kindness, I pray thee, unto me, and make mention of me unto Pharaoh, and bring me out of this house.*"

At this point Joseph had gone through the process of helping one of the two men who had concerns about his dream sort out the destiny issues of his life. It was after interpreting the dream of the first that he made the above request yet the man who had it good failed to remember Joseph. While the man lived his partner was not so lucky, his head was cut off during Pharaoh's birthday ceremony. Joseph languished in prison for several more years: "***Until the time that his word came: the word of the LORD tried him. The king sent and loosed him; even the ruler of the people, and let him go free.***" (Ps 105:19-20).

There was a sister who had a similar experience of serving sacrificially and instead of reward she always received rebuke or condemnation. Her service became inconsequential because her honest actions were always misunderstood. In one instance where she set aside her annual vacation to use it to babysit for a sister who was recently delivered of a baby. On the third month of her volunteer service, the sister being served called her aside and told her never to come again to her house because she believed she came to serve with evil intention.

The false accusation leveled against her was that she was there to serve because she wanted to snatch the husband of her hostess. Even the husband of the accuser was himself shocked because he knew that the sister came to serve genuinely and had no such intention.

However, the accusation stuck and she had to leave the house with heavy heart and bearing the shame of a stigma that she never elicited. This is always the end result of anyone carrying unappreciated destiny. They are always undermined, misunderstood and unappreciated.

12. Limited Destiny

This is an example of a destiny limited in life. No matter how much effort is put into whatever venture he engages in the output or result is not always commensurate with the input. He works like an elephant and reaps the harvest of an ant. In many circumstances it is obvious that there is a stumbling block in his way. It is like an invisible hand repressing or hindering him from moving forward.

What others do with ease and take for granted, is what the man that is limited cautiously spends overtime doing and yet never gets the anticipated result. While the matter seems very confusing to the onlooker, it gets to a point in which the ignorant victim gets discouraged. He believes to some degree that God is partial and the question is always why me? And the more he maintains this stand the more his sufferings grow hooves and horns. Because the thieves come not but to kill, steal and destroy the victim descends from one level of despair to another until he becomes a shadow of himself in discouragement. He loses self esteem and wishes for death than life.

Furthermore, as he turns away from the word, he begins to get isolated and drawn away from the truth. He starts to believe in a lie that he is not better than his fathers and it is better to die than to live. The conviction in instances as these is so strong that it can only take God to intervene and stop the urge for suicide. The limited man is convinced he is no good and death is better than the shame that his life attracts. But where the word of the Lord is allowed to permeate the soul the man fairs better. It may be a slow and tortuous journey but most of the time he is able to get there.

A good example in the Bible is seen in Isaiah 6:1: ***"In the year that king Uzziah died I saw also the LORD sitting upon a throne, high and lifted up, and his train filled the temple."*** (Is. 6:1). As long as Uzziah was alive Isaiah was unable to see the Lord. He was for many years limited by the presence of this king. But suddenly Uzziah died and the supposedly blind prophet began to see. Not only did he see the death of his limitation (Uzziah); he: ***"...saw also the Lord...."*** The glory of the Lord that he saw brought him to a new beginning! Limitation sets its victims back many years. It frustrates and hinders them no matter how hard they try. A good example was a man who left the shores of Nigeria to go to the former Soviet Republic to improve himself academically. He read his Master's and Doctorate (Phd) in Economics and Banking and returned only to face a debilitating joblessness for many years. When it became clear that the path of success commensurate to his academic worth had been blocked, he settled for teaching arithmetic in a primary school. The shame was too overwhelming for a former senior banking official, yet he had no solution to his affliction until God showed up in his case.

Several years after his ordeal began, in his search for freedom, he met with the Lord in a Pentecostal church. Thereafter, the pastor of the church, having received detailed knowledge of what to do from the

Lord about his situation began to show concern. As a result prayer watch was set aside to minister to his needs. In the course of one of the prayer sessions the Holy Spirit showed up and he was asked to go ask his father what he had done to deserve what he was going through.

On getting to the village, his father told him he was angry at him and his three other siblings who abandoned him and went abroad. After, wisely calming his father down with gifts and overtures, he began to bargain effectively for his future. Thereafter, his father took him to the back of the house where he showed him four pots labeled in the names of his four children and each pot bore their placenta in red oil. He profusely thanked his father for forgiving him, and cautiously followed him into the house as he waited for the opportunity to return to the back of the house to uproot the pot in order to secure its content.

As his father proceeded to the house still talking, this man suddenly stopped, jammed the door behind him and ran to the back of the house where he uprooted the pot and ran for his dear life. His 70 year old father, whose reflexes were not as sharp, suddenly realized what his son was up to, and ran after him. But he was no match to his son's speed and agility, and besides he did not have the advantage of time. Hence his effort to stop him was too late.

The man succeeded in taking the pot to Church, and its content was burnt after the covenant on it had been broken through intense warfare. He was within a few months restored to a higher banking position than he used to be before he went abroad for post graduate studies. God answers prayer if only we can pray!

This segment concludes our examination of the identified troubled destinies. The next chapter deals with the solutions to the problems. Because it is useless and unfair to stir up a man's hope and not provide him with needed resources to help him meet his goals, this book puts together detailed do-it-yourself solution that should bring respite to the victims of troubled destinies.

Part IV
Upon Mount Zion……..
"Great is the Lord, and greatly to be praised
in the city of our God, in the mountain of
his holiness. Beautiful for situation………"
– (Ps 48:1-2)

Chapter Seven
Solution to Troubled Destinies

And Jabez was more honourable than his brethren: and his mother called his name Jabez, saying, Because I bare him with sorrow. And Jabez called on the God of Israel, saying, Oh that thou wouldest bless me indeed, and enlarge my coast, and that thine hand might be with me, and that thou wouldest keep me from evil, that it may not grieve me! And God granted him that which he requested. (I Chron. 4:9-10)

Introduction

This chapter provides detailed solution on what to do when confronted with troubles of life. Because it does not make any good sense to point a victim to challenges without proffering needed solutions - this chapter is dedicated to that purpose. This however, is not the total solution but some tips on how to confront the adversaries.

It is necessary to point out that even though people are confronted with varying degrees of wickedness the root cause is the kingdom of darkness. Some people's challenges are peculiar to them when one considers the way they are presented. For this reason, there are no hard and fast rules to approach such situations. However if the basic information is understood the oppressed can through it formulate a plan of action to address his prayer needs. There is a measure of wisdom in doing this.

"Whoso is wise, and will observe these things, even they shall understand the lovingkindness of the LORD." (Psalm 107:43)

Furthermore, the book of Job 5:27 in a similar vein counsels that:

"Lo this, we have searched it, so it is; hear it, and know thou it for thy good."

The need to pursue a solution for one's challenges should be non-negotiable but the fool always tries to explain it away. Even though it is obvious to concerned onlookers yet the victims go about unperturbed by what others see and weep in prayer for mercy on them. When a person confronts his problems by having the determination to know the truth for his good and by searching things out – that person is a wise man. The book of Hosea 14:9 also corroborates this fact:

"Who is wise, and he shall understand these things? prudent, and he shall know them? for the ways of the LORD are right, and the just shall walk in them: but the transgressors shall fall therein."

No matter the storms in our lives or the challenges we face there are suitable solutions from the presence of the Lord. When the children of Israel were confronted with the trouble of Egypt's oppressive rule and the Lord sent plagues upon the land, neither the children of God nor the Egyptians had any clue of what our God could do. Evil pursuers do not always have an inkling of what God has in stock for His people and consequently for their enemies. They always do find out when it is almost too late for them to repent that *"...God is a consuming fire."* (Heb 13:29).

For example, Moses with the rod (authority) of God in his hand, through the power of God caused a lot of havoc in Egypt as we see in Exodus 10:13:

"And Moses stretched forth his rod over the land of Egypt, and the LORD brought an east wind upon the land all that day, and all that night; and when it was morning, the east wind brought the locusts."

The locust destroyed the sustenance of the land and the people were greatly distressed. It took the cry of the Egyptians through Pharaoh for Moses to cry unto God and God told him to lift up his rod again and we see the result in verse 19:

"And the LORD turned a mighty strong west wind, which took away the locusts, and cast them into the Red sea; there remained not one locust in all the coasts of Egypt."

Our God is awesome and is able to do the incredible to make Himself known in any situation. He brought the locust by His power, and through His power He took them away. The overwhelming situations brought by the various plagues unleashed upon them through the servant of God, Moses, took the wind out of their sail and left them thoroughly purged of their pride. They watched Moses change the course of their lives by just watching him lifting up his rod unto situations and they obeyed him. These by no means were terrifying situations that had never been written or read from the pages of any text books up until that time.

God tamed Egypt to the point that when the Israelites were leaving they willingly subjected themselves to be spoiled without any form of resistance. They were too stunned to fight back. All they wanted more than anything was to see the back of the troublesome Israelites who had caused them too much pain and anguish than any nation in the history of their nationhood. Hence, they collaborated with the exiting Israelites in willingly allowing the looting of their belongings.

Another challenging situation is found in the story of the man at the pool of Bethesda, who was said to be lame in his feet and had been by the pool side for thirty eight years. The pool has five porches which are symbolic of grace and it was by a sheep market. Competing for a place in the pool when the angel troubled the water were "......*a great multitude of impotent folk, of blind, halt, withered, waiting for the moving of the water.*" (John 5:3).

The first person to step into troubled water was made whole, yet these handicapped folks found it highly challenging to find their way into the pool because of the competing number of people seeking for opportunity to gain access. These all constituted obvious obstacles in their paths and it was always a stormy situation but no matter how terrible the situation may be there is a day reserved for the freedom of its victim.

The man watched his life ebb away for thirty-eight years without help and no hope of making it out of that place healed until Jesus showed up. Because of the longevity of his case, he was overwhelmed and hence unable to put his act together when Jesus showed up and asked him a simple question that was too good to be true:

"*...Wilt thou be made whole?*" (John 5:6)

The appropriate response to this question should have been either yes or no. But when people had gone through the troubles of life for many years they tend to lose their confidence, devalue themselves and rather become historical. What was the man's answer?

"*.....Sir, I have no man, when the water is troubled, to put me into the pool: but while I am coming, another steppeth down before me.*" V7.

The man simply spoke from his heart – I needed the help of man but I have not gotten one. But in case you do not mind to hang around so that when the angel comes to trouble the water you can assist me to get inside the pool. That was his thought but the Jehovah Rapha, the healer had a different agenda – the helping hand of God. He wanted to put an end to thirty-eight years of hardship – crawling and toiling on the same spot.

While the help of man will fail and fade away the help of God abides forever. God never fails and Has never been known to fail. The Master never followed the man's line of argument, He knew he had suffered there waiting for thirty-eight years and He wanted to close the chapter of prolonged years of infirmity and suffering. Hence, He without further delay whatsoever, **"*... .saith unto him, Rise, take up thy bed, and walk.*"** (Jn 5:8). And that was it. The result was instant.

He does not need any man's permission to do them good because He is the author of good. It is his delight to see the captive set free and that was his superior argument against the Pharisees who were angry when Jesus set the woman bound for eighteen years free. He said to the woman:

"*Woman thou art loosed from thine infirmity*" (Lk. 13:12).

That was the end of the story of infirmity, and she was instantly made whole. The same was true of this man – he was made whole after thirty eight solid years of suffering.

SOLUTIONS TO SATANIC OPPRESSION

1. Recognize there is a problem

The first solution to any given problem is to recognize that it exists in the first place. Many today are in captivity but they have refused to face the reality of the bondage they are in. They spend more time trying to explain it away and convince keen watchers why it has to be so. They sometimes try to tie it with the happenings in their ancestral line and thereby persuade people that it is normal because it runs in the family.

As long as they refuse to see what is happening to them as a problem that required aggressive treatment they will suffer long for nothing in their predicament. The recognition that there is a problem gives the victim the impetus to seek for help on how to put an end to suffering as he discovers the way out.

2. Know why it exists

When the problem is recognized it is equally important to know why it existed and when or how it came into the family. This gives the victim an opportunity to carry out act of repentance or outright spiritual warfare to confront it no matter what the case may be. For example, a man discovered that no member of his family could venture to eat a plate of rice: to them it is like a snail tasting salt, and the result is always catastrophic. Unfortunately for the family, the urge to eat rice was so strong because it was a choice staple food everywhere.

However, one member of this family began an investigation on why they could not eat rice and stumbled at an incredible find. His father many years ago stole a bicycle that belonged to a palm wine tapper. He rode away with it while the owner watched helplessly stranded on the tree. Because the owner could not quickly come down from the tree, the thief gathered speed and ran away. The owner did what only was possible at the moment - he released a curse on the thief. He said **"Anytime you eat the food you enjoy most in your family something would go wrong and you should be rushed to the hospital."** That was it!

The man was told that the only solution to reverse it was to buy a bicycle and take it to the now seventy-five year old palm wine tapper in order for him to rescind the curse. He did and the story changed from that day. This story of restitution paved the way for the deliverance of the family. They knew what to do because they were willing to find out the root cause of the problem. Get some wisdom there.

3. Submit yourself

The next thing to do after getting the required information sufficiently needed for warfare prayers is to first submit to God before resisting the devil. What does it mean? This is to allow the Lord have control of the situation and then give direction as to what to do to get out of it. It is clear that James 4:7 declares:

"Submit yourself therefore unto God, Resist the devil and he will flee from thee..."

Do not go into battle without submitting to God it would be disastrous to do so!

How do I submit? Take time to look at relevant scriptures and meditate. Let the Lord give you the direction for battle. I remember many years ago, when I was confronted with a spiritual challenge. I had a prolonged sickness that was not responding to treatment. I was fine all day till the evening when the sickness kicked in. Then dramatically on Friday through Sunday, I was strong enough to preach, but come Monday the cycle was to begin again. This lasted for three weeks.

It was then it became clear I needed to seek the face of the Lord to confront the affliction. He gave me direction through His word as I confronted the spirit of death. God in his mercy showed up in a dream where the spirit of death in form of a python was pursuing me till the Lord opened to me a way of escape. From that point on I began to give thanks because I knew the battle had been won through submission to the Lord's direction in battle. I was thereafter perfectly healed and made whole.

4. Ask for discernment

It is in the course of submission and waiting that the Lord reveals to you what you need to know and do to strategically prosecute the warfare. Spiritual discernment is a crucial tool in warfare. It minimizes the enemy's position and strategically makes them become vulnerable in warfare. The discerning of spirit gives away the location of the enemy and its strength. It reveals the works of the enemy. This is a gift from the Lord and it is inspired by spending more time praying in the spirit.

If a man prays in an unknown tongue he edifies himself and he builds up his most holy faith. The more you pray in the spirit the more sensitive you are to the leading of his spirit. Actively seek the Lord's face for discernment in whatever situation you find yourself he will walk you through. In fact, it is his delight to do so.

5. Resist the enemy

The mandate of the church is to demonstrate her raw powers to principalities and powers. This is not strange to angels who are aware that God has raised us the church to be change agents because so has the word of God confirmed in the book of Hebrews viz:

"For unto which of the angels said he at any time Thou art my son, this day have I begotten thee?..." "But unto the son he saith thy throne, O God, is for ever...." (Hebrews 1:5, 8).

"For unto the angels hath he not put in subjection the world to come, whereof we speak. But one in a certain place testified, saying, what is man that thou art mindful of him? Or the son of man that thou visitest him? Thou madest him a little lower than the angels; thou crownedst him with glory and honour, and didst set him over the works of thy hands" (Hebrews 2:5-7)

From the above scriptures it is clear that God has put man in charge of situations around him. This is because he has:

"..put all things in subjection under him..." (Hebrews 2:8).

This is the reason the Master could make a vow on our behalf that: *"I will build my church and the gates of hell shall not prevail against him."* (Mt 16:18)

The church from day one is called to wait on the Lord and learn how to do warfare. God wants you to sit at his feet until He makes your enemies your footstool. (Ps 110;1). The enemy must and should be resisted but this is after your submission to the Lord in humility and obedience. There is no other option – you must fight to unseat the enemy having a field day over your inheritance. The only language the enemy understands is the language of force. The Lord and his angels are waiting for you to make the move.

6. *Destroy the powers*

As you resist the enemy do not allow him a breathing space. Bring divine judgment upon them and confine them to the place of divine appointment. Do a thorough work of destroying the foundations of the ungodly that they will not recover strength thereafter. Speak to their altar, the power behind it and the priest of the altar. Command the fire of God to consume them until they become ashes under your feet. Ask that the wind of God blow the ashes away that the enemy would never recover strength to afflict nobody again.

In a nutshell, do your homework and put the enemy to flight. Bring lasting destruction upon them. The word of God in Malachi 4:1 succinctly describes it – you should destroy them till you *"...leave them neither root nor branch."*

7. *Withdraw your name*

Visit the altar of affliction with the words of God that quickens, sharper than any two edged sword and is powerful. Let the word of God bring forth the divine withdrawal of your name from their altars, shrines or covens. Wherever your names may be whether on the land, sea or air let the word locate it and nullify the potency of their powers. Apply the blood of Jesus to your lot and get your freedom from bondage.

Why is this important? Your name bears your nature and is also tied to your strength and blessing. Each time your name is mentioned blessing is released. God gave us indication of this fact by causing the names of Abraham, Sarah and Paul to reflect kingdom purposes. Protect your names from satanic affliction or harm – withdraw your name prophetically.

8. *Pray prophetically*

Prophetic prayer creates an atmosphere for your miracles. Call the things that are not as though they were. Do a prophetic prayer action and claim your victory. What is this? If you know you are stagnated begin to physically take steps of faith as you claim your walk out of stagnation. Tell the devil watch me as I walk on my higher ground! Or watch me as I drive my brand new car. My days of walking barefooted are over. Satan, watch me drive my brand new car to town. Demonstrate your victory with corresponding action.

If it is failure, prophetically take a piece of paper and tear the certificate of failure in your life. Do the same to barrenness, poverty, delay, going round in circles etc. Declare your freedom prophetically and command the enemy to let go. Reclaim every lost ground through violence. Remember the word of God in Mt 11:12

"*Right from the day of John the Baptist and until now the kingdom of heaven suffereth violence and the violent ones taketh it by force.*"

The name of the game is the application of violence. Negotiating your way with a gentleman's approach is an invitation to perpetual bondage and increased suffering. When the right medication is applied to an ailment the end of it is in sight. That is what you are being called to do – take prophetic action.

9. *Reconcile all things back by his blood*

Insist that everything be reconciled with the power of his blood, shed on the cross.

"*And having made peace through the blood of his cross, by him to reconcile all things to himself; by him, I say, whether they be things in earth, or things in heaven*" (Col 1:20).

Appropriate His blood, and let it avail for you in victory as well as for cleansing. Use it as a weapon of offense and defense. Connect with the victory of the cross and the benefits of redemption. For example salvation, healing, deliverance and the possessing of your possessions are all part of the package He acquired for you when He shed his blood on the cross.

Claim the blessings released when He died on the cross for you as He declared right on the cross it is finished. Deal with the handwriting of ordinances and the things contrary to your blessings which He had taken away and nailed to His cross. Blot out the handwriting with His blood and maintain your victory in Him.

10. Claim the victory and give thanks

Give thanks to the Lord and claim total victory over the situation. Be prophetic, direct, certain and convincing. Use appropriate scriptures to declare your victory, for He that has begun a good work in you is able to perfect it. Worship him and rejoice with testimony of His goodness. Maintain your victory by declaring it on a daily basis. Do not give the devil a breathing space.

Be ready to maintain your deliverance by building up your strength spiritually through fasting, praying in the spirit and understanding, reading and meditating on the word, and finally praise and worship. These formidable tools will keep you going strong and your victory is guaranteed in Jesus name.

Chapter Eight
Beautiful for Situation

"Great is the Lord, and greatly to be praised in the city of our God, in the mountain of his holiness. Beautiful for situation, the joy of the whole earth, is mount Zion, on the sides of the north, the city of our great king." – (Ps 48:1-2)

Introduction

Not only is our God great, He is also beautiful for every situation no matter how tough it may be. He is the joy of the whole earth. What makes this to be so is because Mount Zion is the place of deliverance, holiness and the possessing of our possessions. Several instances in the Bible have proved how beautiful our God is. Several testimonies of troubled destinies are almost everywhere in the Bible to prove His faithfulness in turning situations around. Many impossible situations have become possible and witnessed inspiring outcomes through God's favor.

For example there was a man filled with a Legion of demons in Mark Chapter 5 verses 1-20. The destiny of this man had been vandalized until he met Jesus. But the Lord the man of war set this man free from debilitating bondage that had consigned him amongst the dead for many years. The power of His word was available to silence the powers of darkness that took forceful residence in the life of that man. He puts a sudden end to years of living in the tombs and dwelling amongst the dead. That day life and death had a head-on collision and it was death that succumbed. The man's situation thereafter became so beautiful that he was found sitting at the feet of the master in his sound mind. What a wonderful testimony!

In spite of this heart-warming testimony and turn around in the life of this man set free from satanic strongholds, the elders of the city did not find what Jesus did amusing in any way whatsoever. They weighed all that happened to the demoniac against the cost of 2000 pigs that drowned as a result and concluded that Jesus must be an economic saboteur. It did not matter to them that the son of Abraham who had made his habitation amongst the tombs was now free: *"...sitting, and clothed, and in its right mind."* (Mk 5:15). The one thing that came to their minds in their ignorance was to give him immediate deportation order out of their community: *"And they began to pray him to depart out of their coasts"* (Mk 5:17)

One should not be surprised that these people opted to send Jesus away because of what happened to their swine. If one is aware of the history of Gadara, and its founding fathers one should by no means be surprised. The people of Gadara by historical connection came from the tribe of Gad. Their actions toward the Lord were only the revelation of their response to the seed their ancestors sowed. The background story was that during the wilderness journey to the promise land the tribes of Gad and Reuben told Moses:

"...if we have found grace in thy sight, let this land be given unto thy servants for a possession, and bring us not over Jordan" (Num 32:5).

Can you imagine their request? God took them out of Egypt to bring them into the promise land yet they asked not to go over Jordan because the land they were was good for cattle. The land of Canaan was God's plan for them but in their bad judgment they requested to opt out of God's promise. Their forefathers exercised bad judgment and they too had begun to follow in their steps. So it was not a surprise when they asked Jesus to leave their coasts. It is true that a seed will bear after its own kind.

This incident was a pointer to the fact that a curse must have been at work in the lives of the tribes of Reuben and Gad to have made the unimaginable request to stay back. This is because ordinarily it does not make sense! This in fact elicits the need for a brief investigation into their past – what happened?

It was discovered that the destinies of both Reuben and Gad were affected by their father's pronouncements in Genesis 49:3-4:

"Reuben, thou art my firstborn, my might, and the beginning of my strength, the excellency of power: Unstable as water, thou shalt not excel; because thou wentest to thy father's bed then defiledst thou it..."

What a profound utterance, *"thou shalt not excel"* and he did not.

And for Gad it was just one liner that was so potent enough to pull him out of the way of victory, and he could not wriggle out of its strangulating effect.

"Gad, a troop shall overcome him: but he shall overcome at the last." V19.

Gad had no business teaming up with Reuben to stay back from entering the promise land but for the effect of the curse. Laboring under the weight of the curse the tribe of Gad continued to make bad judgment to the point in which they began to rear unclean animal, - swine. Therefore when the demons prayed Him, the Lord Jesus, let us go into the herd of swine He allowed it to show His displeasure at the decision of the children of Gad in staying back to rear swine. In one day 2000 swine perished.

In the same chapter, another ugly situation had an encounter with Jesus, just as He left the people of Gadara. He was met by one of the rulers of the synagogue known as Jairus, whose little daughter was terminally ill and he wanted Jesus to come lay hands on her that she may be healed. But in the meantime, Jairus did not know his daughter had died. Yet, the Master knew and He was ready to make the ugly situation become beautiful. The destiny of this twelve year old had been snuffed out. She died in her prime by the hand of evil. But she was soon to encounter Jesus, so that death again should give way to life. (Mk5:21-23, 35-43). When Jesus showed up, in spite of the commotion in Jairus' house, death gave way to life and resurrection was the result. She was raised from the dead and the story of her life changed. Snuffed out destiny was turned around from death to life.

It is interesting to point out, that earlier in the day someone hijacked her own miracle and delayed the Master from going to attend to Jairus' daughter. This was a woman who had suffered unceasing blood flow and loss for 12 years. The ugly situation had rendered her thoroughly abused by many. The summary of her life was that she:

"..had suffered many things of many physicians, and had spent all that she had, and was nothing bettered, but rather grew worse." (Mk 5:26)

But when she heard about Jesus her story changed. She said to herself if I could but touch the helm of His garment I would be made whole and that was exactly what happened. She desperately pushed through the obstacle - the crowd and eventually managed to touch the helm of His garment then something happened. Her blood flow stopped immediately and Jesus felt virtue leave him. That day abused destiny was turned around and she was free form bondage.

There are many ugly situations that the master made beautiful that space is not enough to declare. The situations mentioned above were all terrible yet the Master made the situations become very beautiful. Is your situation ugly or terrible? Come to Jesus on the mountain of Zion he would change your story to glory. He has never been known to fail, He would not fail in your situation – He would make it become beautiful. Jabez heeded the call and his stagnated destiny was touched. Not only did God answer his five point prayer, he was made more honorable than his brethren. How did he achieve this? He called on God and made his request known (I Chron. 4v10). He prayed and God granted him his requests.

Ruth also found help when she turned to the Lord to help her in the impossible situation she found herself. Orpah her sister in-law had turned back but Ruth maintained her loyalty and she found help. The situation of Ruth was so ugly that one wonders where was she going to start? Her mother-in-law Naomi was equally in a worse shape – she lost her husband and two sons. It was a house of sorrow – everyone lost someone and was in deep grief for their losses.

Beyond her ugly situation, Ruth was disadvantaged in many ways which made her matters worse. Number one, she was not a maiden. So she stood the risk of not getting appropriate suitors to fulfill her dream or goal in life. Two, from the Jewish perspective she had even more profound disadvantages - She was a gentile. A gentile had no place in God's plan up until that time. Three, she was a Moabite, and which Moab was under a curse (Dt. 23:2-3). Fourth, she was a woman. A woman does not have much relevance or matter in Jewish tradition. Yet in spite of all these challenges, God turned her situation around (Ps. 126:1-2).

Briefly enumerated in the following pages are the milestones of blessings God gave Ruth on her return to Bethlehem Judah with Naomi. Ruth's journey from truncated and frustrated destinies to one beloved and favored by God and men are itemized below. Her journey through faith helped her to re-connect with a colorful destiny. It is possible for you too if you can believe!

A. Ruth's Milestones to Favored Destiny

1. Time of Barley Harvest

We see from the scriptures that both Ruth and Naomi got to Bethlehem Judah at the time of the Barley harvest. They arrived at the nick of time to be partakers of a harvest they never sowed. In a nutshell God made a way for them to enjoy the harvest they did not sow (Ruth 1:22). This is nothing but unsolicited favor. God arose on their behalf.

Even though Naomi asked the people to call her Mara (bitterness) yet God had other plans. Her bitterness suddenly became sweet when God showed up in her situation. Their lives picked up again because God decided to make their truncated destinies blossom again. He gave them a new beginning and something to rejoice about – a harvest in the midst of debilitating lack.

2. Provision of home

Both women arrived without hope and help of any form but God gave them a home of their own. It was from this home that they began to put together the broken pieces of their lives. He knows our needs even before we ask or yearn for it. He is the mighty God the great I am. A hopeless situation turned around when hope showed up with joy. They left the land of Moab with joy and they were led forth into the harvest with peace, and the mountains and the hills broke forth before them and the tree of the field clapped their hands (Is 55:12)

3. Divine leading

While Ruth was looking forward to another path of destiny to thread with fear, God had better plans and she was led to that portion of the field that belonged to Boaz a kinsman of Elimelech (Ruth 2:3). There she labored diligently and found sustenance through the favor and the mercy of God.

4. Job Confirmed

Boaz was curious when she saw a beautiful damsel unknown to him laboring on his field. As expected he enquired about her and he was told that she was:

"*....the Moabitish damsel that came back with Naomi out of the country of Moab*" (Ruth 2:5-6).

Furthermore, the reapers gave wonderful account of her hard work tarrying in the field from morning till evening except for a short time of break for refreshment which pleased Boaz tremendously. He immediately confirmed her job the same day and commanded the reapers to show her favor and unusual privileges reserved for the beloved. (Ruth 2:8-9)

5. Grace

This gentile woman was overwhelmed by the avalanche of blessings and kindness showed her by Boaz that she could not hold back. The Bible reveals to us that: "*..she fell on her face, and bowed herself to the ground, and said unto him, Why have I found grace in thine eyes, that thou shouldest take knowledge of me, seeing I am a stranger?*" (Ruth 2:10)

She could not hide her surprise. Some blessings demand the question why? This was one of them. In response, Boaz hinted her it was her character or conduct that was the seed that brought the harvest of fruits of kindness she received.

"And Boaz answered and said unto her, It hath fully been shewed me, all that thou hast done unto thy mother in law since the death of thine husband: and how thou hast left thy father and thy mother, and the land of thy nativity, and art come unto a people which thou knewest not heretofore." (v11).

Her sacrifice forced divine attention and attracted grace in her favor. Such sacrificial decisions always command divine attention that equally draws God's speedy allocation. All the person needs to do is to discover his place, and remain committed there, grace will show up.

6. Favor

Ruth was not satisfied with just receiving grace in her sight, she requested for favor. Even though I am not one of your beloved ladies, you have comforted me by your words, and have spoken kindly to me therefore: *"....Let me find favour in thy sight, ..."* (V13).

The lesson here is: do not settle for less keep asking until you reach your goal. The Lord has more than enough to meet your needs only if you can ask. He is waiting for you to do so instead of complaining. Convert your complaints to prayer and pray till something happen. This one targeted request for favor speedily opened further doors of opportunity to her that knocked her off her feet. It was unbelievable release of favor that was beyond her imagination. It was more than enough blessings:

"And Boaz said unto her, At mealtime come thou hither, and eat of the bread, and dip thy morsel in the vinegar. And she sat beside the reapers: and he reached her parched corn, and she did eat, and was sufficed, and left. And when she was risen up to glean, Boaz commanded his young men, saying, Let her glean even among the sheaves, and reproach her not: And let fall also some of the handfuls of purpose for her, and leave them, that she may glean them, and rebuke her not. So she gleaned in the field until even, and beat out that she had gleaned: and it was about an ephah of barley. And she took it up, and went into the city: and her mother in law saw what she had gleaned: and she brought forth, and gave to her that she had reserved after she was sufficed." (v14-18)

7. She was Focused

One thing that was clear about Ruth was that she was focused. She never tried to deviate from her goal of finding a path to settling down no matter where the Lord leads. She was not willing to choose for herself but she left the choosing to the Lord who for this reason began to work in her favor. In the first instance, the Lord led her to Boaz's farm land and she was committed to the leading. She did not for once begin to feel he was an old man, but was willing to accept God's choice for her life. When Naomi heard who it was that she worked for she was exceedingly glad and she said:

"...Blessed be he of the LORD, who hath not left off his kindness to the living and to the dead. And Naomi said unto her, The man is near of kin unto us, one of our next kinsmen." (V20)

8. Obedience

Ruth also demonstrated unusual obedience in the circumstance by adhering to the counsels of Boaz and principally that of Naomi. She obeyed the instruction of Boaz to remain in his farmland and work. This Naomi confirmed and advised her that it is good for her: *".. to go out with his maidens, that they meet thee not in any other field."* (v22) The bible confirms in the following verse:

"So she kept fast by the maidens of Boaz to glean unto the end of barley harvest and of wheat harvest; and dwelt with her mother in law."

What followed thereafter was the strategic scheme to get the attention of Boaz in a morally and cultured way. Being part of the culture, Naomi schooled her on what to do because she was aware of the tradition of the people. Ruth followed each counsel with diligence (Ruth 3:1-5):

"And she went down unto the floor, and did according to all that her mother in law bade her." (v6)

When Boaz discovered Ruth's application of the culture and tradition he was more than impressed as well as interested in the outcome because:

"...all the city of my people doth know that thou art a virtuous woman" (v11).

He expressed his appreciation in glowing words and further reassured her of the process her request would take as there was a more near kinsman than him in the picture. If the man refused to *"..do the part of a kinsman"* then he would do it." (v13).

9. She was Blessed

Her focus and obedience to counsel brought her patriarchal blessing that positioned her in the path of her goal.

"And he said, Blessed be thou of the LORD, my daughter: for thou hast shewed more kindness in the latter end than at the beginning, inasmuch as thou followedst not young men, whether poor or rich." (v10).

Here was a gentile woman in the path of becoming a mother in the lineage of David through to Jesus. Yet, it never occurred to Boaz's Jewish instinct of deep prejudice that wait a minute what do I have to do with this woman yet he pushed on in his desire to marry her. God was at work.

10. Enjoyed Abundant Supply

What followed the spiritual pronouncement was material blessing: Ruth enjoyed abundant supply. According to her account she said Boaz told her: *"..Go not empty unto thy mother-in-law."* (v17).

As a result she got six measures of barley to the bargain and went into the city unto her mother- in-law. On hearing what transpired, Naomi assured her:

"Sit still, my daughter, until thou know how the matter will fall: for the man will not be in rest, until he have finished the thing this day." (v18).

With good counsel winning a war is certain, and a person's rise to greatness is equally assured if he is surrounded by good counselors. Such was the blessing that Ruth enjoyed.

11. Inheritance Redeemed

True to his promise, when the near kinsman refused to do the part of the kinsman unto Ruth, Boaz did in the sight of the elders at the gate.

"And Boaz said unto the elders, and unto all the people, Ye are witnesses this day, that I have bought all that was Elimelech's, and all that was Chilion's and Mahlon's, of the hand of Naomi. Moreover Ruth the Moabitess, the wife of Mahlon, have I purchased to be my wife, to raise up the name of the dead upon his inheritance, that the name of the dead be not cut off from among his brethren, and from the gate of his place: ye are witnesses this day. And all the people that were in the gate, and the elders, said, We are witnesses.." (Ruth 4:9-11).

12. Husband

The redemption of the inheritance of Elimelech and his generation by Boaz automatically gave him the legal right to marry Ruth. God visited Ruth and gave her a husband who happened to be in the lineage of Christ. God positioned her because of her commitment and determination to remain faithful to Naomi. Boaz became the husband of Ruth and they prayed for Boaz and said may:

"..The LORD make the woman that is come into thine house like Rachel and like Leah, which two did build the house of Israel: and do thou worthily in Ephratah, and be famous in Bethlehem: And let thy house be like the house of Pharez, whom Tamar bare unto Judah, of the seed which the LORD shall give thee of this young woman. So Boaz took Ruth, and she was his wife:…" (Ruth 4:9-13).

13. God gave her a Child of Destiny

The Lord finally blessed her with a child. Her marriage to Boaz gave her a future and hope. Anywhere the lineage of Jesus is mentioned she would be mentioned because she became the mother of: *"…Obed: he is the father of Jesse, the father of David."* (Ruth 4:17)

14. Generations linked to David through to Jesus

The generations from Boaz and Ruth produced Obed who became the father of Jesse, and Jesse the father of David until the Lord Jesus.

"And Salmon begat Booz of Rachab; and Booz begat Obed of Ruth; and Obed begat Jesse; And Jesse begat David the king; and David the king begat Solomon of her that had been the wife of Urias; So all the generations from Abraham to David are fourteen generations; and from David until the carrying away into Babylon are fourteen generations; and from the carrying away into Babylon unto Christ are fourteen generations. " (Matt 1:5-6, 17)

B. HOW DID SHE GET HERE?

i) She offered herself with rugged determination

The right attitude that Ruth adopted to confront the challenges she faced prepared her for success. She did not consider herself but was willing to sacrifice her life by offering what was left of her future to a culture and tradition she was not particularly deeply familiar with. Her contact with the living God, even though superficial, was sufficient enough to convince her she must give her life to Him in order to enjoy the benefits He would offer. It was therefore no wonder when she said:

"Intreat me not to leave thee, or to return from following after thee: for whither thou goest, I will go; and where thou lodgest, I will lodge: thy people shall be my people, and thy God my God: Where thou diest, will I die, and there will I be buried: the LORD do so to me, and more also, if ought but death part thee and me." (Ruth 1:16-17)

Ruth's resolution commanded divine respect and the attempt to convince her otherwise would have been an uphill task. Even Naomi did not understand or rather comprehend the depth of Ruth's conviction hence she kept pressing her to go back. When it became clear to her that: *"... she was stedfastly minded to go with her......"* she left her. (v18)

It was the same selfless attitude that Boaz saw in her that he was convinced that Ruth was a woman of virtue. This caused him to resolve to do whatever it would take to meet her request for redemption. So, when Ruth asked him why are you so kind to me, knowing that I am a stranger?

"And Boaz answered and said unto her, It hath fully been shewed me, all that thou hast done unto thy mother in law since the death of thine husband: and how thou hast left thy father and thy mother, and the land of thy nativity, and art come unto a people which thou knewest not heretofore. The LORD recompense thy work, and a full reward be given thee of the LORD God of Israel, under whose wings thou art come to trust." (Ruth 2:11-12)

ii)   ***She gave her Resources***

Ruth seemed to me a divine enigma! She was a gentile woman who had no direct relationship with the God of heaven but demonstrated the principles of the kingdom. This woman after she had gleaned brought the proceeds of her labor to her mother-in-law.

"So she gleaned in the field until even, and beat out that she had gleaned: and it was about an ephah of barley. And she took it up, and went into the city: and her mother in law saw what she had gleaned: and she brought forth, and gave to her that she had reserved after she was sufficed."

She had not only given herself she also gave her resources. The principle of giving was strong in her conduct and this paved the way for her breakthrough.

iii) She was obedient to Divine Counsel

Ruth was a great learner and a desirable mentoree. She was committed to do what she was taught to do and she did it very well. Many have walked this path and bungled it simply because of disobedience or the spirit of arrogance. The Lord had begun a work on her, and had worked in her and now was working with her. She recognized this and was wise to tag along with divine counsel that Naomi gave her.

"And she said unto her, All that thou sayest unto me I will do. And she went down unto the floor, and did according to all that her

mother in law bade her. And when Boaz had eaten and drunk, and his heart was merry, he went to lie down at the end of the heap of corn: and she came softly, and uncovered his feet, and laid her down." (Ruth 3:5-7)

iv) She was discreet about the process

Ruth was so discreet in the application of the counsel she got that you will know that she was a woman endowed. While she was willing to follow tradition she was not ready to throw away her female pride.

"And she lay at his feet until the morning: and she rose up before one could know another...." (Ruth 3:14).

She also demonstrated discipline in her conduct and approach. She did not have an alarm to wake her up but she did wake up in good enough time because she had trained herself to be so disposed. Some would have needed a bedlam to wake up.

v) She was open

Ruth did not hide anything from Naomi, she was transparently open to her on all accounts. This disposition granted her continuous favor as she made progress on her path to destiny. So when she met with her she declared all that transpired between her and Boaz without leaving anything out.

"And when she came to her mother in law, she said, Who art thou, my daughter? And she told her all that the man had done to her. And she said, These six measures of barley gave he me; for he said to me, Go not empty unto thy mother in law." (Ruth 3:16-17).

Ruth imbibed truth and she demonstrated it. Her honest disposition should also be acknowledged. She should be a good example for young married women who desired peaceful relationships with their mother-in-laws.

vi) She was patient, submissive and humble.

Finally Ruth was patient, submissive ad humble. Never did she for once demonstrate anxiety of any kind. She had her peace settled with God and she reaped the reward. Her willingness to learn and give herself totally to a right cause procured for her an enviable destiny. From troubled to favored destiny she refused to be confined to the pages of history just like Orpah did. She connected with the people of God, dwelt in their land and God the blessings the land gave. Ruth is an example for many women to emulate. A virtuous woman in her own class!

C. As You have Heard So shall you See

I want to conclude with the following prophetic verse of scriptures in Psalm 48 verse 8. *"As we have heard, so have we seen in the city of the LORD of hosts, in the city of our God: God will establish it for ever. Selah"*.

My prayer for you is that you have read this book, as well as heard the prophetic message in it. It is a personal message to you from the Lord. Just as you have heard the testimonies and breakthroughs, so shall you also see your own too come to pass. In the city of our God, it will come to pass. Because upon mount Zion there shall be deliverance, holiness and the house of Jacob shall possess their possessions. You do not have to do anything about it, just find and maintain your place in Him - He will show up and perfect everything. For every encounter we have in Christ there is a price. Hear what I Peter 5:10 declares: *"But the God of all grace, who hath called us unto his eternal glory by Christ Jesus, after that ye have suffered a while, make you perfect, stablish, strengthen, settle you."*

Have you paid your price in suffering in Him for a while? Have you faced some challenges because of his name? Do you see it as something you want to abandon and walk away from? No. Do not do that. God is placing on you the mark of Christ. His grace is sufficient for you because He is the God of all grace. The grace to walk with, in and for Him is available as we trust him to do so.

Your suffering for a while will procure for you maturity – *"...that is make you perfect."* Maturity comes through overcoming challenges. He that quits in the face of challenges lacks understanding. The growth that emanates from challenges prepares a person for excellence. He is thus strengthened and made fit for the master's use as a vessel of honor.

In Romans Chapter 5, the following words of encouragement best articulate the issue of suffering under discussion. It is important you know:

".... that tribulation worketh patience; And patience, experience; and experience, hope: And hope maketh not ashamed; because the love of God is shed abroad in our hearts by the Holy Ghost which is given unto us." (v3-5)

The fruits of suffering for a while produce maturity, and maturity establishment, and establishment strength, and strength settlement. It is all in this order. While you go through the pains associated with the maturing process do not complain – be patient. This will work out patience in you that is beyond understanding. Patience will acquire for you experience and experience hope. This is the hope that does not make ashamed. This is because the love of God is shed abroad in your hearts through the power of the Holy Ghost.

While I thank you for standing by me as we walk through this process together, I want to congratulate you for the victory that will follow this process. My prayer for you is that as you have heard so shall you see, in the city of our God, God will establish it. Amen.

Other books by the Author

i) Fighting Your Way To Victory - (*Principles of Victory over stubborn problems*)

ii) Smashing the Gates of the enemy – *through strategic prayers.*

iii) The Secrets of prevailing in Prayer

iv) Dealing With Generation Wasters

v) The 10 Dangerous Possessions

Contact

To Contact Taiwo Ayeni

For speaking engagements

Please write or call

E: mail –taayeni@rehobothbministries.org

Or

Rehoboth Bible Ministries Inc

2304 Oak Lane., 3A Suite 7,

Grand Prairie, Texas, 75051

Phones: 972-602- 1837

972-742- 7365

Website: www.rehobothbministries.org

About the Book

Help for troubled Destinies begins with examination of what God did for us in the beginning, the foundation of empowerment laid for us to excel, where we missed it and God's follow-up rescue plan. This background approach clearly shows us that we were empowered to succeed from the beginning as revealed in man's encounter with God in Genesis Chapter 1:28. There God blessed man and He gave him five faith commands to pursue: be fruitful and multiply, replenish the earth, subdue it and have dominion.

From this perspective the book goes on to express the fact that because man had been positioned to excel he ought not to experience troubled destinies. Several of these were examined for the readers' attention and solutions to them also proffered. It concludes with testimonies that God is beautiful for every situation.

About the author

Pastor Taiye Ayeni as he is fondly called, met with the Lord in his final year at the University of Lagos, Akoka, where he graduated with a Bachelors of Science combined honors degree in Mass Communication, Sociology and Psychology.

Since knowing the Lord in 1983, he has been privileged to serve Him in various capacities. He is the Minister in Charge of Rehoboth Bible Ministries Inc, based in Grand Prairie Texas, USA and a Senior Lecturer at the Gethsemane Prayer Ministries International' Prayer School, with its headquarters in Ibadan, Nigeria.

He serves as a Minister at the Household of Faith, of The Redeemed Christian Church of God (RCCG) Arlington, Texas, USA where he and his family worship. He is in the United States of America on mission for Christ, a trained Chaplain and graduate of Advance Leadership and Pastoral School of Christ For The Nations Institute (CFNI) Dallas and Long Ridge Writers Group, in Connecticut. He is widely traveled on speaking engagements within and outside the country in the course of ministry work.

He lives with his wife Abidemi, Rereloluwa (son) and Oreoluwa (daughter) in Grand Prairie Texas.

9 781449 058555